Serbia

Kosovo

Bulgaria

• *Skopje*

Republic of
North Macedonia

ia

Greece

*This map reflects the present-day geographic boundaries of North Macedonia.
Over the centuries, however, borders have shifted a great deal and the
population of ethnic Macedonians spans across boarders into the many
surrounding villages and towns.

*Aegean
Sea*

MACEDONIA

THE COOKBOOK

MACEDONIA

THE COOKBOOK

KATERINA NITSOU

Photography by Oliver Fitzgerald

KITCHEN PRESS

First published in the US in 2021 by
Interlink Books, Massachusetts

First published in the UK in 2021 by
Kitchen Press
1 Windsor Place
Dundee
DD2 1BG

Distributed in Australia and New Zealand by David Bateman Ltd

A catalogue record for this book is available from the British Library
ISBN 978-1-9163165-6-0

Printed and bound in Korea
10 9 8 7 6 5 4 3 2 1

*To my mother, Linda, and to my
teta Sophie for all their support
and guidance, and to Oliver whom I
could not have done this without.*

CONTENTS
Sodržina

PREDGOVOR PREFACE

As a Macedonian woman, I have learned the importance of food. As a chef, I have learned how to refine that food. My maternal grandfather was a chef in his own restaurant and, among others in my family, very inspirational to my culinary career.

In the late 1920s, during the first major wave of Macedonian immigration to North America, my grandfather travelled to Canada at the age of twenty-two. His father had died when he was nine, and as the only man in the family, he believed he was leaving home to seek a brighter future. Little did he know he was heading straight into the Great Depression. Upon arrival, he did not speak a word of English but he was committed to making Canada his new home. In Toronto, he united with fellow Macedonians to navigate the perils of his new home, managing to survive by eating bean soup and cabbage stew.

Working odd jobs, he eventually saved enough money to open what became a very successful restaurant in the heart of downtown Toronto. He served a combination of traditional Macedonian fare and North American–style diner food. He had a wonderful ability for maximising flavour, while maintaining the simplicity of what he was cooking.

Throughout his life and career, he didn't just cook. He developed methods and reasons for the "whys" and the "hows" of food. Although my grandfather was not formally trained, he understood his craft immensely well and certainly set a masterful standard of quality. He was meticulous when it came to cooking, and this devotion to perfection was the first lesson I learned in respecting the integrity of the ingredient.

My father's family did not leave the "old country" to move to Toronto until the 1960s. My father's two sisters moved to Toronto first, as teenagers, and my father hoped that he and his parents and younger brother would one day be reunited with them. Having studied at university in Greece, my father was able to come to Canada as a landed immigrant quite quickly. His parents and younger brother followed in 1972, and his family was able to realise its dreams of being reunited. When I was growing up, my entire extended family lived in Toronto, and it was through my father's side that I learned to enjoy large family gatherings and the cooking that went with them. The weekends and holidays of my childhood were loud and colourful, and filled with people. During these gatherings, I watched my mother, grandmother, aunts and cousins working together in the kitchen to put together a feast—in particular, my father's sister Sophie, who was also a restaurateur in Toronto and has an incredible knowledge of the way food was prepared in the village and the appropriate protocol when it comes to which foods are to be served and for which occasions. My mother and my aunt both played integral roles in developing my love of cooking and hosting. It is something they both did so effortlessly, and which brought so much joy to our family.

I've always loved the family style of eating—the sharing of large platters around the table and the way the flavours complemented each other beautifully on the plate. The great thing about Macedonian cuisine is that regardless of what combination of dishes is being served, it all seems to work and make sense as a single, bountiful spread. I have been diligent in maintaining the true essence of Macedonian cuisine in this book. I have also updated and simplified some of the recipes so they are easy for modern home cooks to master. I began writing this book before I started my culinary training at Le Cordon Bleu where I was able to refine my techniques. My internship at the Los Angeles Times Test Kitchen, however, truly helped redefine my ability to write recipes.

I chose to write a Macedonian cookbook because it is the food I know best and the food that I love most. I also want to teach and share with others a bit about this glorious part of the world. I have always believed, as most chefs do, that the best way to learn about any country or culture is through its food and, more importantly, through its kitchens.

Through my research for this book, I realised that there is much abundance in Macedonian cuisine, much more than the few dozen recipes that were the staples in my home growing up. While writing, there were many times in my own kitchen that I felt deeply connected to my family and my ancestry simply because I was preparing food that they had been making for centuries. A celebration of a culture, this book is a journey into a culinary world that is modest, simple and honest.

INTRODUCTION

The food of Macedonia is rustic and unassuming, guided by the land and perfected by the people. It embodies a culinary tradition that has been deeply rooted and passed down through generations, while being inspired along the way by the surrounding cultures that have left their footprint on the region.

The people of Macedonia date back to ancient times. Before our common era, Macedonia was vast and spread over much of the southern Balkan Peninsula. So when referencing Macedonia in this book, I mean the geographic area of the Kingdom of Alexander the Great, which Macedonians inhabit. Presently the country is called North Macedonia, although for centuries Macedonians have inhabited the lands that surround the country's current border.

But food has no borders, and over many centuries, this geographic area was occupied and culturally influenced by the Byzantine Empire, the Christian Orthodox Church, the Turkish Ottoman Empire, the Balkan Wars and the First and Second World Wars. Macedonians have inevitably assimilated some of the culinary and cultural practices, ingredients and flavours these cultures brought with them that are now staples in the Macedonian kitchen. Most notably, they brought spices such as cinnamon and mahleb (made from the ground seeds of a sour cherry tree) from Turkey and the Middle East, rice from the Orient and olive oil and citrus from the Mediterranean.

The cultivation of Macedonian cuisine has evolved over thousands of years as a reaction to what grew locally, as well as to trade that was taking place. Even though borders have changed drastically over the last two thousand years, the spirit and heart of the Macedonian people still pulses among the rolling mountains and valleys. With Serbia and Kosovo to the north, Bulgaria to the east, Greece to the south and Albania to the west, Macedonia remains well regarded as a centre for agriculture among its neighbouring countries. There are cultural crossovers, not only between the surrounding countries but also from the neighbouring villages and towns.

The terrain of Macedonia is undulating. Colourful fruits and vegetables grow in the mountains and valleys; livestock and freshwater fish are abundant. With micro-growing conditions within Macedonia and a long history of rudimentary farming practices, the groundwork was set for the cuisine to be highly adaptable to whatever grew well and in abundance that year. The origins of our recipes are quite ancient, yet continue to flourish and are still staples today. Our dishes have been perfected in Macedonian homes for centuries and passed down from generation to generation, each family or region taking a slightly different approach. Luckily, it is not an overly complicated way to cook. There are no special tools or procedures that are necessary to accomplish these dishes. The goal of each dish is to simply achieve balance, and to highlight the quality and integrity of the ingredients.

Today, Macedonia's landscape still remains quite rustic and rural, with much of its industry focused on agriculture. The rich fertile land, sunshine and temperate climate makes agriculture a necessary and natural choice. The selection of the fruits, vegetables and herbs grown in the countryside are bountiful and robust with flavour. Macedonia is also known for its quality of grapes, which makes for award-winning wines that are now beginning to receive global acclaim. Wine history in Macedonia can be traced back to around 1300 BC, at least 700 years before grapevine origins in France. Rakija is also a very popular fruit spirit that can be made with plums or apricots, but in Macedonia it is typically made with white grapes and anise. Peppers are perhaps one of the most popular ingredients in Macedonia, with a multitude of varieties but most notably the heirloom Rezha Macedonian pepper. They are incorporated into many of the recipes, or simply roasted with oil, garlic and salt and enjoyed as a standard accompaniment to meals. Ajvar (page 27), a dip made with roasted peppers, is another national speciality. Beans play a huge role in the canvas of the Macedonian cuisine and are highly regarded for their quality. Tavche Gravche (Traditional White Bean Stew, page 177) is Macedonia's national dish.

Many of the Macedonians I know and grew up with are from rural villages. My father's village is called Rula, and my mother's village is Bresnitza. Both are within the Lerin (Florina) region of present-day northern Greece. In the last century, my family, along with thousands of other Macedonians, emigrated to countries like Canada, Australia and the United States. I was born and raised in Toronto, and although I did not grow up in Macedonia, the Macedonian culture was very prevalent in my own life and upbringing. Macedonian was my first spoken language, and our social interactions as children were shared with our very large extended family who all held the memories of their motherland dear to their hearts. This love of culture was imparted to us as children through dance, art, music—and, of course, food. True to the adaptative nature of the cuisine, we were brought up with traditional Macedonian food that was altered to utilise what was available in North America. Instead of the Rezha pepper, we used red peppers or banana peppers. Hospitality and family gatherings were at the core of our childhood, and through this, we learned about our traditions. Overall, our culture is quite social, and the gathering of people is a big part of daily life. These gatherings were never formal. They were open to all, and the ethos was always, "Whatever we have, we will share it with you." This way of thinking made gatherings pleasurable because there was no pressure to make hosting complicated.

Macedonian cities and villages are filled with flourishing markets, bustling street cafés and restaurants with large patios that spill out onto the street. Macedonians love going out for a rashetka (outing) to have a drink and snack at a kafeana (café) and to listen to music and socialise. Religious and non-religious festivals are also popular in the cities and villages. Huge gatherings of people celebrate with live music, dancing, food and drinks. Growing up in Toronto, we celebrated the same way. There would be winter dances and summer picnics nearly every weekend. These were big events, often with hundreds of people attending.

Yet to sample the true essence of Macedonian culture, one must dig deep into the home, where you capture the authenticity of the food and the stories of the Macedonian people. Home is where men and women come together to enjoy the fruits of their labours through recipes that have been handed down and perfected over many generations. Capturing this was at the heart of creating this book.

THE MACEDONIAN CULTURE

The Macedonian culture is rich and deeply rooted in tradition with a charming tapestry of music, dance, dress, celebrations, rituals and food. With so many different cities and villages, it is only natural that there are different approaches and variances to the customs and traditions. Each city or village collectively shared in the same core traditions but often with slightly different approaches.

My interpretation of the culture is based on the small villages my parents are from. Even though they were neighbouring villages and only about six kilometres away from each other, there were quite distinct differences in their dialect, way of dressing and technical skill sets. For example, my mother's village was a little more modern and the common trade was stone masonry, whereas my father's village was much more agriculturally guided. The majority of Macedonians are Christian Orthodox. Although there are many other religions being practiced, Orthodox Christianity remains the main religion of Macedonians. I touch on this because religious celebrations are deeply woven throughout the culture. Weddings, births, baptisms and funerals are milestones in many cultures and specific foods are prepared for each. For example, at weddings a very large ornate round bread called Pogacha (Braided Rich Bread, page 202) is made and decorated with braided dough and sesame seeds. After the ceremony, the bride and groom each hold one end of the bread and tear it apart. Whoever tears off the largest piece is meant to "rule the household". The bread is then portioned out and each guest at the wedding must have a piece for good luck.

In the Christian Orthodox tradition, there are saints' name days, which celebrate the feast days of different saints. Babies are often named after a saint, and their saint's name day is celebrated similarly to a birthday. It is a big celebration, and for Macedonians, name days are much anticipated annual events. The day is typically celebrated in the home and an offering of Kozinak (Easter Bread, page 206) and pchenica (sweet wheat berries) along with cookies, cakes and red wine are given to visiting guests and family. "Srekna Slava" or "Sreken Imenden"—salutations meaning "Happy Saint Day" or "Happy Name Day"—are shared for good luck.

Macedonians can also be quite superstitious. Because superstitions are the storytelling and the legacy of every civilisation, many superstitions have survived in Macedonia and are still believed in today. They may vary from family to family and city to city, but whether believed in or not, they provide insight into the Macedonian way of life. One of the superstitions from my mother's village was that it was considered very bad luck, and an act of greed, to be holding food in both hands at the same time during meals. Another that many believe in is the "evil eye". My grandmother was really adamant about covering babies with loose muslin when in public so strangers couldn't see them. She also believed in putting a bit of salt on babies' tongues to protect them from the "evil eye". Superstitions in Macedonia run deep—an entire book could be devoted to this topic alone!

Traditional Macedonian music dates back centuries, and it was highly influenced by the Ottoman Empire. It is folk music that over the years took on Oriental elements to create a distinct sound. Macedonian folk music is heavily vocal and created by a small band of musicians that play instruments like a gaida, which is similar to a Scottish bagpipe, a tapan, which is a double-headed bass drum, a tambura, a stringed instrument like a mandolin, and a kaval, which is like a large flute. As the music modernised, key instruments in Macedonian music now include the clarinet, guitar and traditional drums. Currently, there is a new generation of young Macedonian artists who are creating pop and rock music, but there is still a deep love for the traditional folk music, even among younger generations. Younger artists are also incorporating the traditional folk songs, as well as new lyrics, into their own melodies. The repertoire of Macedonian music is very expressive, as it touches on all aspects of human experience, including love, family, loss, war and playful humour.

Much of the music is upbeat and suitable for dancing. With the traditional music, there are specific dances that correspond to each song. Traditional Macedonian dancing involves quite intricate footwork, where people hold hands and dance in an anticlockwise circle, called an oro. One of Macedonia's most popular songs is "Makedonsko Devojče", written and composed by Jonče Hristovski in 1964 about a Macedonian maiden and her beauty. Truly beautiful, it is a popular choice for the bride's oro at her wedding. At Macedonian weddings, each family member is honoured with an oro that they get to choose and lead, as a sign of respect to that person.

Another popular Macedonian custom at weddings is the bieshetoe oro, "pig dance", which is performed at the reception. In this dance, members of the wedding party arrive with bottles of wine and carrying a beautiful roasted suckling pig. They bring the pig to the future godparents (best man and maid of honour) and tauntingly demand payment for the pig. The godparents adorn the platter with money, and the pig is then taken and portioned for all the guests. The money goes to the happy couple as a sign of good fortune and prosperity for their future. This custom is always performed with the theme of festivity and joy, as the guests clap along.

Traditional Macedonian dress is another way you can see the distinct differences between villages and regions. Clothing was handmade, mainly from cotton and wool.

Bright in colour, it was quite elaborate in decoration, embellished with sequins, embroidery and coins. Women would wear a cotton or linen tunic, usually white or ivory. A woollen sleeveless overcoat would be worn over the tunic, something like a waistcoat that would tie in the front, and a woollen apron would be worn over that. Other items, like sleeves and high socks, would be added on in the colder months, and all would be beautifully decorated. Women typically wore a schamia, or scarf, around their heads, which would be tied behind the head for younger girls, or under the chin for older women. The men's attire was a little less elaborate but also included a tunic, along with fitted trousers and, depending on the region of Macedonia, a skirt over the top of the trousers and either a waistcoat or jacket. Both women and men wore pinci, shoes made from pig's hide.

When I was a young girl, my grandmother gave me a traditional outfit from my father's village that she had made. She made one for all of her granddaughters from the original fabrics she had loomed in the village, and before she passed away she gave me a child's dress for my daughter Kalina.

Macedonian culture is as rich as it is diverse. It is an ancient civilisation that has endured centuries of conquest and war, yet Macedonians are lighthearted, joyful and generous people who take great pride in their roots. Strong cultural ties and traditions have been practiced for centuries and are still embraced today.

MEZZE

Small Plates

MEZZE
Small Plates

In the Macedonian culture, mezze is the first offering. It usually involves a combination of small tastes to enjoy at your leisure. It could be as simple as cheese, olives and bread, or a more elaborate spread of small nibbles that pair well with alcoholic or non-alcoholic drinks. Sometimes, for casual gatherings or a light lunch, traditional mezze is all you need. A selection of a few small dishes, a glass of wine and great conversation is my favourite way to eat and entertain.

LUTI PIPERKI
SPICY PEPPERS

Roasted peppers are at the core of Macedonian cuisine and the first thing that comes to mind when I think of Macedonian food. They appeared on our table alongside nearly every meal. Although this recipe calls for spicy peppers, it can also be made with sweet peppers of any variety that you find in your grocer's or market.

8–10 whole hot
  banana peppers
1 teaspoon extra-virgin
  olive oil
1 garlic clove, very finely sliced
1 teaspoon chopped parsley
½ teaspoon sea salt

Roast the peppers over a charcoal grill or a gas flame until the skins are completely charred and blistered. Alternatively put them under a hot grill (directly on the rack or on a baking sheet lined with parchment paper), rotating them every 15 minutes until charred, 30 to 45 minutes.

Place peppers in a paper bag or heatproof container. Seal and set aside for 20 minutes until cool.

Peel off the skins, keeping the peppers intact.

In a large bowl, gently toss the peppers with the oil, garlic, parsley and salt.

Arrange on a serving dish.

MASLINKI
OLIVES

Olives are a popular mezze. Although they don't commonly grow in the Macedonian region, they have become a staple in the cuisine. For guests, I love to spice up my olives right before serving them. Slightly roasting them warms the natural oils and softens their flavour.

900g unpitted mixed olives in oil, drained

1 tablespoon extra-virgin olive oil

2 garlic cloves, finely minced

2 teaspoons lemon zest

1 teaspoon finely chopped fresh dill

½ teaspoon freshly ground black pepper

Preheat the oven to 230°C.

Rinse the olives under cold running water. Drain and pat them dry.

Arrange the olives on a baking sheet in a single layer and roast for 10 to 15 minutes until sizzling.

In a medium bowl, toss together the olive oil, garlic, lemon zest, dill and black pepper to make a marinade.

Toss the hot olives in the marinade and stir to coat them evenly.

Let cool slightly before serving.

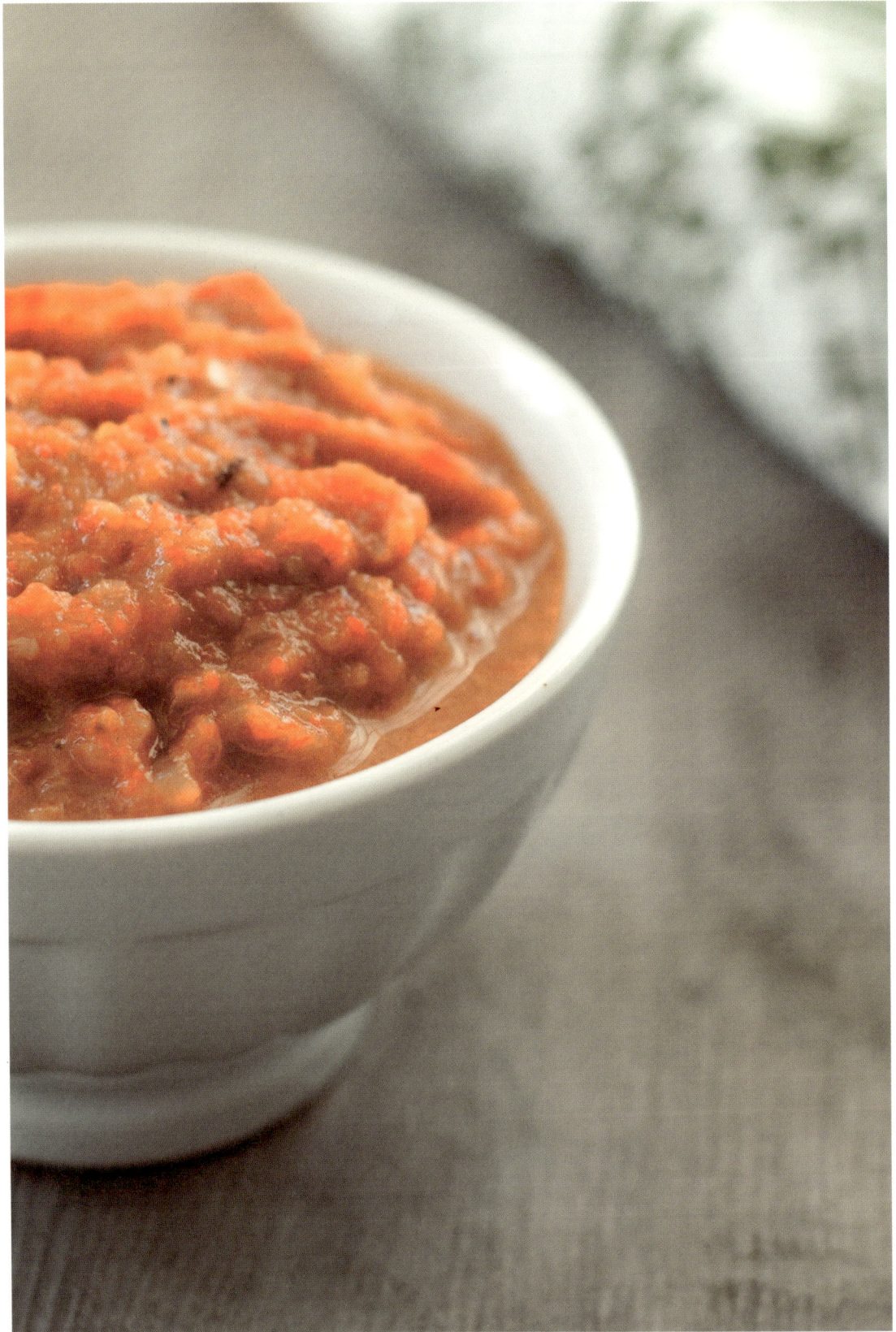

AJVAR
ROASTED RED PEPPER & AUBERGINE DIP

Ajvar is popular throughout the Balkans, often served as a condiment for grilled meats or simply with bread and cheese. Macedonians take their Ajvar very seriously. In the autumn, when red peppers are in season in the region, families get together outdoors with dozens of pounds of peppers to make enough jars of Ajvar for the winter months to come. It is quite labour-intensive, and the work is typically rewarded with a meal of grilled sausages at the end of the day. Ajvar is made by roasting the peppers and aubergines over open flames and, traditionally, grinding them by hand, but using a food processor is much easier.

1 medium aubergine

6 red peppers

60ml extra-virgin olive oil

1 medium onion, chopped

3 garlic cloves, finely chopped

½ teaspoon crushed chillies

1 tablespoon red
   wine vinegar

Juice of 1 lemon

½ teaspoon sugar

1½ teaspoons sea salt

½ tablespoon freshly ground
   black pepper

Using a fork, pierce the aubergine skin a few times all around.

Roast the peppers and aubergines over a charcoal grill or a gas flame until the skins are completely charred and blistered. Alternatively put them under a hot grill (directly on the rack or on a baking sheet lined with parchment paper), rotating every 15 minutes until charred, for 30 to 45 minutes.

Place the roasted vegetables into a paper bag or a heatproof container. Seal and set aside for 20 minutes until cool.

Peel off and discard the skin and stems from the aubergine and peppers, and remove the pepper seeds. Coarsely chop the flesh and set aside.

In a large stockpot, heat the oil over medium heat and sauté the onion until very soft, about 4 minutes. Add the garlic and red pepper flakes and cook, stirring constantly, for 2 more minutes. Remove from the heat.

Add the vinegar, lemon juice, sugar, salt and black pepper to the pot, and stir in the pepper and aubergine pulp.

Using an immersion blender or food processor, blend the mixture to a coarse paste with a slightly chunky texture. Be careful not to completely purée the mixture. Store in a glass container in the refrigerator.

PINDJUR
ROASTED AUBERGINE DIP

Pindjur is similar to Ajvar (Roasted Red Pepper and Aubergine Dip, page 27) in how it is made. These recipes were important in Macedonian homes to maximise the harvest and preserve the ingredients that were in abundance. Even growing up in Toronto, my entire family had lush, abundant gardens in their backyards and we would get together in the autumn to preserve what was grown. We always had jars of Pindjur and Ajvar stored in the fridge. Both dips are delicious served as a condiment to grilled meats, or simply with cheese, olives and toasted flatbread.

2 large aubergines
¼ onion, very finely grated or
   minced
½ garlic clove, grated
Juice of ½ lemon
2 teaspoons sea salt
60ml extra-virgin
   olive oil

Using a fork, pierce the aubergine skin a few times.

Roast the aubergines over a charcoal grill or a gas flame until skins are completely charred and blistered. Alternatively, preheat the oven to 230°C and roast the aubergines on a baking sheet lined with parchment paper, rotating every 15 minutes until charred, for 30 to 45 minutes.

Meanwhile, in a small bowl, mix together the onion, garlic, lemon juice and salt. Cover and refrigerate for 20 minutes for the flavours to meld.

Place the roasted aubergines in a paper bag or heatproof container. Seal and set aside for 20 minutes until cool.

Remove the skins and stems, and coarsely chop the aubergine flesh. Transfer to a food processor and add the onion mixture.

With the food processor running, slowly pour in the oil. Purée until smooth.

Transfer to a dish and refrigerate for at least 2 hours before serving.

KISOLO MLEKO
SO PECHEN
YOGURT WITH GARLIC, CUCUMBER & DILL
LUK

Roasting the garlic is not traditional for this dip but, as a child, I always found the raw garlic to be too pungent. My family believes that garlic cures all, so they amped it up any chance they could. I found that roasting the garlic and adding a little sour cream gives this dip richness and a mild, but well-rounded flavour. It is a wonderful accompaniment to grilled meats, and I also love it with Pitulitsi So Zeleni Tikvichki (Courgette Fritters, page 37).

1 whole garlic bulb, unpeeled

1½ teaspoons extra-virgin olive oil

1½ teaspoons sea salt

½ cucumber, unpeeled, grated

240ml plain full-fat Balkan yogurt (or any full-fat yogurt)

240ml full-fat sour cream

1 tablespoon coarsely chopped fresh dill

Juice of ½ lemon

Preheat the oven to 180°C.

Cut about 1cm off the top of the garlic bulb. Drizzle the cloves with ½ teaspoon of the olive oil and sprinkle with ½ teaspoon of the salt. Place the bulb in the centre of a small sheet of foil and wrap it completely. Bake for 35 minutes, until soft. Remove from the oven and let cool.

Place the grated cucumber in a clean tea towel and squeeze out as much liquid as possible.

In a large mixing bowl, combine the yogurt, sour cream, 1 teaspoon olive oil, 1 teaspoon sea salt and the cucumber and dill.

Squeeze out the roasted garlic cloves onto a chopping board and use the back of a fork to mash the garlic to a paste. Add the mashed garlic to the yogurt mixture. Add the lemon juice and stir to incorporate.

Transfer to a dish and refrigerate for at least 2 hours before serving.

LUK I OREV SOS

GARLIC & WALNUT DIP

Walnuts grow in abundance in many regions of Macedonia. Growing up, we always kept a big bucket of whole walnuts in their shells in a dark cupboard. My mother would make this recipe in a pinch if she needed something to offer to unexpected guests. We usually serve it with freshly made Pita Na Skara (Grilled Flatbread, page 211). This dish is also a great way to use up day-old bread.

5 garlic cloves, coarsely chopped

2 tablespoons red wine vinegar

1 tablespoon sea salt

60g chopped walnuts

450g day-old white bread, crusts removed, coarsely chopped

120ml extra-virgin olive oil, plus extra for serving

In a food processor, blend the garlic, vinegar and salt to a paste. Use a spatula to scrape down the sides. Add the walnuts and pulse until the mixture becomes mealy (be careful not to over-process).

Place the bread in a colander in the sink and pour about 480ml hot water over it. Using your hands, squeeze out any excess water from the bread and transfer it to the food processor.

With the machine running, slowly pour in the oil. Purée until creamy.

Transfer the dip to a dish and refrigerate for at least 2 hours, before serving with a drizzle of olive oil.

LUKANKI
GRILLED SAUSAGE SKEWERS

Whenever we had company over, we served sausages. My father would head out early Saturday mornings to pick up fresh sausages from a friend who made them. There is nothing better than freshly made sausages, and we looked forward to them all day. My mother would poach them early in the day so they could be grilled just as guests were arriving. You will need 12 metal skewers or pre-soaked bamboo skewers for this dish (soak bamboo skewers for 20 minutes).

4–6 mild or spicy
  Italian-style sausages

2 medium onions,
  cut into wedges

2 red peppers, cut into bite-size
  pieces

1 tablespoon extra-virgin
  olive oil

½ teaspoon sea salt

Juice of ½ lemon

Using a fork, prick each sausage about 3 times on each side.

Fill a medium stockpot with warm water, add the sausages, and bring to a gentle simmer over medium heat. Let the sausages poach for 10 minutes. Drain the sausages and allow to cool.

Place the onions and peppers in a large bowl. Drizzle with the olive oil and sprinkle with the salt. Toss to coat.

Diagonally slice the sausages into 2.5cm pieces.

Preheat your grill or a stovetop grill pan to medium-high heat.

Thread the sausage pieces onto skewers, alternating them with the onion and pepper pieces, making sure you have at least 2 pieces of each ingredient on each skewer.

Grill the skewers for about 5 minutes on each side or until the sausages brown and the onion and peppers are tender and nicely charred.

Transfer to a serving dish and drizzle with lemon juice. Serve immediately.

PITULITSI SO ZELENI TIKVICHKI

COURGETTE FRITTERS

This recipe is something we make on lazy weekend afternoons and is one of my husband's favourites. The addition of feta adds a bit of salty sharpness to the mild courgette. Serve them with Kisolo Mleko So Pechen Luk (Yogurt with Garlic, Cucumber and Dill, page 31) on the side.

600g courgette (3 medium), grated

1 medium starchy potato, such as Maris Piper, peeled and grated

4 spring onions, thinly sliced

115g feta cheese, grated

40g plain flour

2 teaspoons finely chopped fresh dill

¼ teaspoon paprika

1 tablespoon sea salt

½ teaspoon freshly ground black pepper

2 eggs, beaten

Vegetable oil, for frying

In a large mixing bowl, combine the courgette, potato, spring onions and cheese.

In a separate small bowl, whisk together the flour, dill, paprika, salt and black pepper.

Sprinkle the dry ingredients over the courgette mixture and toss to coat. Fold the eggs into the courgette mixture until fully incorporated.

In a large sauté pan, heat 2 tablespoons of vegetable oil until it begins to shimmer.

Without crowding the pan, drop large spoonfuls of courgette mixture into the oil and gently press down with the back of the spoon to flatten. Fry the fritters for 5 to 6 minutes on each side until golden brown, then transfer to a plate lined with paper towels to drain excess oil. Repeat with the remaining courgette mixture, adding about 2 tablespoons of vegetable oil to the pan for each batch. Serve immediately.

PIPERKI SO
OVCHJO

ROASTED PEPPER & FETA CHEESE DIP

SERENJE

This dip is so addictive. Slightly spicy, salty and somewhat sweet all in one. I have been a little conservative with the amount of red chilli pepper flakes in this recipe but feel free to add more if you like it spicier. This dip is great alongside grilled meat dishes, but served with a loaf of bread, it can be a complete meal as it is.

8 red peppers
150g feta cheese, grated
1 tablespoon extra-virgin
  olive oil
1 teaspoon freshly
  squeezed lemon juice
½ teaspoon crushed chilli
  flakes
1 teaspoon sea salt
1 teaspoon freshly ground
  black pepper

Roast the peppers over a charcoal grill or a gas flame until the skins are completely charred and blistered. Alternatively put them under a hot grill (directly on the rack, or on a baking sheet lined with parchment paper), rotating them every 15 minutes until charred, for 30 to 45 minutes.

Place the roasted peppers in a paper bag or heatproof container. Seal and set aside for 20 minutes until cool.

Peel off the skins and remove the stems and seeds.

Transfer the peppers to a food processor and pulse a few times to break them up. Add the feta cheese, oil, lemon juice, chilli flakes, salt and black pepper. Pulse until the mixture starts to become creamy, leaving some texture.

Chill before serving.

KOFTINKA
BITE-SIZE MEATBALLS

This is my father's secret recipe. The milk makes the meat really tender and the mint adds freshness. Now that I live away from home, whenever I travel back to visit, these are always on my list of foods I want my father to make upon my arrival. They are delicious served with fresh bread and a selection of dips, like Kisolo Mleko So Pechen Luk (Yogurt with Garlic, Cucumber and Dill, page 31), Ajvar (Roasted Red Pepper and Aubergine Dip, page 27), and Piperki So Ovchjo Serenje (Roasted Pepper and Feta Cheese Dip, page 38).

450g lean minced beef

60g dried breadcrumbs

4 spring onions, thinly sliced

2 eggs, beaten

60ml whole milk

1½ teaspoons sea salt

1 teaspoon freshly ground
  black pepper

2 tablespoons finely chopped
  fresh mint

1 tablespoon extra-virgin olive
  oil, plus extra for greasing

Preheat the oven to 230°C and grease a baking sheet with olive oil.

In a large bowl, gently mix all of the ingredients until evenly incorporated. Be careful not to overwork the meat.

Roll the meat mixture into small balls, about 2.5cm in diameter.

Arrange the meatballs on the greased baking sheet and roast for 20 to 25 minutes until cooked through.

Remove from oven and transfer the meatballs to a plate lined with paper towels to drain excess fat.

Arrange on a serving dish.

SARMI SO
STUFFED VINE LEAVES
LOZOV LIST

This recipe may seem a little intimidating but it is actually quite easy. Sarmi make fantastic leftovers. My mother always doubled the recipe so we had them on hand in the fridge. I now use jarred vine leaves, but growing up, we used fresh grape vine leaves from my grandmother's garden. (If you are lucky enough to have access to fresh vine leaves, soak them in boiling salted water for about a minute to soften them before using.)

450g jar of vine leaves
Boiling water
Juice of ½ lemon

In a large stockpot, bring 2 litres of water to a boil. Carefully remove the leaves from the jar and place them in the boiling water. Simmer for 2 minutes. Carefully remove the leaves using tongs and drain. Set aside.

FILLING

900g lean minced beef
225g minced pork
1 teaspoon extra-virgin
   olive oil
1 medium onion, grated
1 egg
240ml low-salt chicken stock
1 tablespoon finely chopped
   fresh dill
½ teaspoon paprika
90g long-grain white rice
2 teaspoons sea salt
1 teaspoon freshly ground
   black pepper

In a large bowl, gently combine the filling ingredients.

Line the bottom of a stockpot with 4 or 5 leaves, overlapping them to create a base. This is a good way to use torn leaves. Place one leaf on your work surface, smooth side down. Trim the stem off at the base of the leaf and place about a tablespoonful of filling just above it. Fold each side of the leaf over the filling, and roll from the bottom to make a roll tight enough that it is secure, but not so tight that it will tear when the rice cooks. Repeat until all the filling has been used.

Arrange the stuffed grape leaves close together in the bottom of the pot in concentric circles, stacking them if needed. Pour in just enough boiling water to submerge the rolls. Squeeze in the lemon juice and place a smaller heatproof plate or pot lid on top of the rolls in the pot, to provide a gentle weight so they do not unravel during cooking. Simmer, covered, over medium-low heat, for 1 hour or until the rice is cooked.

Remove from the heat and let stand for an additional 10 minutes, covered. Carefully remove each roll and place on a baking sheet with a rack in order to drain any excess liquid. Serve warm or cold.

PRZHENI
FRIED SMELTS
TSIRONI

Nothing says summer for me like freshly fried smelts. I have memories of sitting in the summer sun with my father and uncles, playing chess or cards, and snacking on these crisp little fish with a cold beer. I love the light crust you get from the flour and seasoning; this simple treatment means you can really taste the delicate fish. I prefer the mild flavour of smelts for this recipe, but if you cannot find them, you can use sardines or herring.

24 fresh or thawed smelts, fins trimmed, gills, head and innards removed

60g plain flour

2 teaspoons sea salt

1 teaspoon freshly ground black pepper

2 teaspoons paprika

60ml vegetable oil

1 tablespoon coarsely chopped fresh parsley

1 lemon, cut into wedges, for serving

Rinse the smelts and pat them dry.

In a shallow baking dish, mix together the flour, salt, black pepper and paprika. Coat each fish in flour mixture.

In a large sauté pan, heat the oil until it begins to shimmer.

Place the smelts into the oil one at a time, being careful not to overcrowd the pan. Fry the fish for 2 to 4 minutes on each side to develop a golden crust. You may need to fry in batches.

Using a slotted spoon, transfer the cooked fish to a plate lined with paper towels to drain excess oil.

Garnish with chopped parsley and lemon wedges. Serve immediately.

PALACHINKI SO PRAZ

LEEK PANCAKES

This is such an impressive dish to serve to guests. My Aunt Niki would often make it for us when we visited, and it was much anticipated. As a child, it was almost like having a slice of cake, but savoury. The combination of sautéed leeks, feta and ricotta is a delicious contrast to the subtly flavoured pancakes.

PANCAKES

125g plain flour

2 eggs

120ml whole milk

240ml water

½ teaspoon sea salt

1 tablespoon unsalted butter, melted, plus extra for greasing

FILLING

1 tablespoon extra-virgin olive oil

2 large leeks (white and light green parts only), diced

1 garlic clove, minced

240g ricotta cheese

150g feta cheese, grated

120ml hot water

1 teaspoon sea salt

In a blender, combine all of the pancake ingredients and blend for 10 seconds until smooth. Chill in the refrigerator for 30 minutes.

Meanwhile, make the filling: In a large sauté pan, heat the olive oil over medium heat. Add the leeks and garlic and sauté until softened, 3 to 4 minutes. Remove from the heat and transfer to a mixing bowl. Whisk in the cheeses, hot water and salt to form a paste. Set aside.

To make the pancakes: Heat a nonstick frying pan over medium heat and lightly grease with butter. Pour in just enough batter to cover the bottom of the pan and rotate the pan to form a thin layer of batter across the base. Cook until the batter becomes dry on top and the edges separate from the pan, 2 to 4 minutes. Using a spatula, gently peel away the edges and flip the pancake over. Cook the other side for an additional 2 to 4 minutes, then transfer to a plate. Re-grease the pan with butter if needed and repeat until all of the batter has been used. You should have 6 to 8 pancakes.

Place a pancake on a flat serving plate. Smear a large spoonful of filling (about 60ml) over the surface of the pancake, then top with another pancake. Repeat the layering process until all of the pancakes and filling have been used, making sure you finish with a pancake.

Slice into wedges and serve.

SALATA

Salads

SALATA
Salads

Geographically, Macedonia is on about the same latitude as the Tuscan region of Italy, and it is a country rich in agriculture. There are many different Macedonian salads for every season, and all are simple and easy to make. In the sunny summer months, peppers, tomatoes and cucumbers are commonly used in salads. The winters are cool and crisp, so heartier ingredients like beetroot, potatoes, carrots and beans are favoured. You will notice that all of these salads are dressed very simply, just enhancing the flavour and beauty of the ingredients.

MAKEDONSKA SALATA

MACEDONIAN MIXED SALAD

*This simple garden salad is bright and fresh, and a vibrant
addition to any meal. We have this salad regularly in our family.
I love the crunch you get from the celery and radishes, paired
with the softer texture of the lettuce and tomatoes.*

1 small seedless cucumber

1 large or 2 small heads of
   loose leaf lettuce, chopped
   into bite-size pieces

2 medium tomatoes,
   sliced into wedges

1 medium celery stalk, thinly
   sliced on the diagonal

1 small carrot, grated or
   peeled into thin strips

2 spring onions, thinly sliced

2 radishes, finely sliced

DRESSING

3 tablespoons extra-virgin
   olive oil

1 tablespoon red wine vinegar

½ teaspoon sea salt

½ teaspoon freshly ground
   black pepper

Peel the cucumber and cut it in half lengthwise. Slice diagonally into
1cm thick slices. Place in a large salad bowl and add all of the other salad
ingredients.

In a small bowl, whisk together dressing ingredients.

Just before serving, pour the dressing over the salad and gently toss to coat.

LETNA
SUMMER SALAD
SALATA

*This classic Macedonian salad is often known as "village salad". Simple
ingredients come together in a harmony of refreshing flavour, perfect for
summer meals. My favourite part is reaching the bottom of the bowl, where the
creamy salty feta, velvety olive oil and tart vinegar mix with the juices from
the vegetables, making a golden liquid that is perfect for dipping (we call this
mackni). So be sure to serve this salad with plenty of crusty bread. I like to peel
the cucumbers in stripes for a bit of contrast and to soften the texture of the
sometimes-thick skin.*

4 medium tomatoes,
 sliced into wedges

1 cucumber, skin peeled in
 stripes and sliced into 6mm
 rounds

½ small red onion, very
 thinly sliced

1 red pepper, cut into
 bite-size pieces

75g feta cheese, shaved

DRESSING

3 tablespoons extra-virgin
 olive oil

1 tablespoon red wine vinegar

1 teaspoon finely chopped
 fresh oregano

¼ teaspoon sea salt

½ teaspoon freshly ground
 black pepper

Place the salad ingredients, aside from the feta, in a large serving bowl.

In a small bowl, whisk together the dressing ingredients.

Pour the dressing over the salad and gently toss to coat.

Chill in the refrigerator for about 10 minutes before serving.

Top with shaved feta cheese.

SALATA SO TSVEKLO

BEETROOT SALAD

Beetroots grow really well in Macedonia but are really only used for salads, rather than in hot meals. My Aunt Mary made this salad almost every day when I visited her in Australia. Her garden was full of beetroot, and I always think of her when I make this salad. She sometimes used mint or coriander in place of the parsley and either works well.

4 medium beetroot, scrubbed

½ medium red onion,
   finely sliced

2 tablespoons chopped
   fresh parsley

DRESSING

1 tablespoon extra-virgin
   olive oil

1 teaspoon red wine vinegar

1 teaspoon freshly squeezed
   lemon juice

¼ teaspoon sea salt

¼ teaspoon freshly ground
   black pepper

Trim the tops and bottoms off the beetroot, leaving the skins on.

Prepare a stovetop steamer with boiling water and steam the beetroot for about 30 minutes, or until tender and cooked through. Remove from the heat and allow to cool for 10 minutes.

Peel off the skins. Slice the beetroot in half lengthwise and then cut them into 1cm wedges.

Transfer to a large bowl and add the onion and parsley.

In a small bowl, whisk together the dressing ingredients.

Pour the dressing over the beetroot and gently toss to coat.

Transfer to a serving dish. Serve warm or cold.

KOMPIROVA

POTATO SALAD

SALATA

This hearty salad is traditionally served at weddings in Macedonia (probably because it goes well with rakija, the popular anise-flavoured liqueur). Growing up, it was a staple at family picnics because it travelled so well and could stay unrefrigerated for a few hours. It is a great way to use potatoes outside of the traditional stews and soups. I've used red potatoes here because I love how silky they are. They have a tougher skin that helps to hold their shape but you could really use any potato variety you like.

2kg medium red potatoes (about 12), cut into equal-size chunks

1 tablespoon sea salt

In a large pot, cover the potatoes with water and 1 tablespoon of salt, and bring to a boil. Reduce the heat to medium and simmer for about 10 minutes, or until the potatoes are tender but not falling apart. Drain in a colander and transfer to a large bowl.

DRESSING

3 spring onions, finely sliced

2 tablespoons finely chopped fresh dill

Juice of 1 lemon

60ml extra-virgin olive oil

1 teaspoon sea salt

1 tablespoon lemon zest

In a small bowl, whisk together the dressing ingredients.

Pour the dressing over the potatoes and gently toss to coat.

Transfer to a serving dish. Serve warm or cold.

SALATA SO
PECHENI
PIPERKI

ROASTED SWEET PEPPER SALAD

Roasted sweet peppers are used in many Macedonian dishes. Sweet bell peppers are best for this salad because of their thicker flesh. My parents often made this salad to use up slightly overripe peppers in an effort not to waste them.

2 red peppers
2 yellow peppers
2 orange peppers
Fresh parsley leaves,
   for garnish

DRESSING

1 garlic clove, minced
1 tablespoon extra-virgin
   olive oil
1 tablespoon freshly
   squeezed lemon juice
¼ teaspoon sea salt
¼ teaspoon freshly ground
   black pepper

Roast the peppers over a charcoal grill or a gas flame until the skins are completely charred and blistered. Alternatively put them under a hot grill (directly on the rack, or on a baking sheet lined with parchment paper), rotating them every 15 minutes until charred, for 30 to 45 minutes.

Place peppers in a paper bag or heatproof container. Seal and set aside for 20 minutes until cool.

Peel off the skins, keeping the stems and seeds intact. Set a colander over the sink and drain the peppers for 20 minutes. Coarsely chop the peppers and place them in a large bowl.

In a small bowl, whisk together dressing ingredients.

Pour the dressing over the peppers and gently toss to coat. Arrange on a serving dish and garnish with parsley.

SALATA SO KRASTAVITSI

CUCUMBER SALAD

I love using a combination of cucumber varieties to give this salad a bit of dimension and texture. You can really use any kind you like, but if you're using anything other than English or Persian cucumbers, I would recommend removing the seeds before slicing, since these can be quite bitter.

1 English cucumber, skin peeled in stripes, sliced into 6mm rounds

6 Persian cucumbers, skin peeled in stripes, sliced into 6mm rounds

½ small red onion, finely sliced

6g fresh mint, finely chopped

75g feta cheese, grated

DRESSING

1 tablespoon extra-virgin olive oil

½ tablespoon red wine vinegar

¼ teaspoon sea salt

In a large bowl, combine the cucumbers, onion and mint.

In a small bowl, whisk together the dressing ingredients.

Pour the dressing over the salad and gently toss just to coat.

Transfer to a serving dish and top with grated feta cheese.

PATLIDJAN SALATA

ROASTED AUBERGINE SALAD

This is such a great salad and could very easily be a meal in itself. It can be served warm but I actually prefer it cold. I love to add the fresh mint when the ingredients are just cooked because the heat wilts the mint ever so slightly and softens its texture.

2 aubergines, peeled and chopped into 2.5cm cubes

4 tablespoons extra-virgin olive oil

1 red bell pepper, diced into 1cm pieces

1 green pepper, diced into 1cm pieces

1 tomato, seeds removed, diced

1 garlic clove, finely grated or minced

Juice of ½ lemon

2 tablespoons chopped fresh mint, for garnish

Sea salt and freshly ground black pepper

Preheat the oven to 180°C.

Place the aubergines on a baking sheet. Drizzle with 2 tablespoons of the olive oil and sprinkle with 1 teaspoon of sea salt. Toss to coat.

Roast the aubergines for 40 minutes, turning them over halfway through, until tender and golden brown.

Meanwhile, heat 1 tablespoon of oil over medium heat and sauté the peppers until just tender, 4 to 5 minutes.

In a large heat resistant bowl, mix together the peppers, tomato, garlic, the remaining tablespoon of olive oil, the lemon juice and ½ teaspoon of salt. Add the aubergines and toss to coat.

Transfer to a serving dish and sprinkle with black pepper and fresh mint.

SALATA SO PCHENICA

WHEAT BERRY SALAD

In the region of Macedonia my family is from, wheat berries are an important part of local traditions. For funerals, unsweetened wheat berries are served to all attendees, alongside bread, cheese and wine. For births and baptisms, wheat berries are sweetened and decorated with dried fruits and sweets. Growing up, we all loved wheat berries and my mother made this recipe for us in big batches, since it keeps well for several days in the fridge. I use whole hard red wheat berries, but you can use other types, or even spelt or farro (just adjust the cooking time accordingly).

370g whole wheat berries

4 medium tomatoes, halved

½ red onion, finely sliced

6g fresh parsley, finely chopped

75g feta cheese, grated

DRESSING

60ml extra-virgin olive oil

Juice of ½ lemon

1 tablespoon red wine vinegar

½ teaspoon sea salt

½ teaspoon freshly ground black pepper

In a medium stockpot, combine the wheat berries and 1.4 litres of water. Bring to a boil over high heat, then reduce the heat to medium-low and simmer, uncovered, for 2½ hours. Drain and rinse with cold water. Set aside in a colander to let dry.

Preheat the oven to 150°C.

Place the tomatoes cut side up on a baking sheet and roast for 2½ to 3 hours until the flesh has shrivelled but not completely dried out. Remove and set aside to cool.

Finely chop the cooled tomatoes and place them in a large bowl. Add the cooked wheat berries, onion and parsley.

In a small bowl, whisk together the dressing ingredients. Pour the dressing over the salad and gently toss to coat.

Transfer to a serving dish and top with the feta cheese.

SALATA SO LUBENITSA
WATERMELON SALAD

This salad is the epitome of summer. Growing up in a Macedonian household, we very rarely ate watermelon without feta cheese on the side. Sweet, juicy, salty—it is the perfect combination. Flash-pickling the onions mellows their flavour so they complement the watermelon, feta and mint instead of competing with them.

¼ red onion, very finely sliced

Juice of ½ lemon

1 tablespoon extra-virgin olive oil

½ watermelon, chopped into bite-size cubes

1 tablespoon finely chopped fresh mint

75g feta cheese, shaved

In a small bowl, mix together the onion, lemon juice and olive oil. Set aside to marinate for 10 minutes.

Place the watermelon in a large bowl and add the marinated onion. Gently toss to coat.

Transfer to a serving dish and top with the mint and feta cheese.

MORKOVA SALATA

CARROT SALAD

This was the first salad I can remember eating. My father would make it for my sister and me when we were kids, and we would get so excited when he'd let us help grate the carrots.

8–10 carrots, peeled
   and grated

30g chopped walnuts

40g raisins

DRESSING

60ml plain full-fat Balkan
   yogurt (or any full-fat yogurt)

2 tablespoons extra-virgin
   olive oil

1 teaspoon freshly squeezed
   lemon juice

½ teaspoon lemon zest

½ garlic clove, finely grated
   or minced

1 teaspoon sea salt

Place the carrots in a large bowl.

In a small bowl, whisk together the dressing ingredients.

Pour the dressing over the carrots and gently toss to coat.

Refrigerate for at least 1 hour before serving. Garnish with the walnuts and raisins.

ZELKOVA
CABBAGE SALAD
SALATA

I love this fresh side dish. I've never been a fan of the classic American-style coleslaw; I much prefer the simplicity of this light dressing. I dress the salad about an hour before I want to serve it to soften the crispness of the cabbage. I use white cabbage in this recipe since it is more common in Macedonia, but you could easily make this salad with red, Savoy or a combination of different cabbages.

1 white cabbage, cored, outer layers removed, finely shredded

DRESSING
60ml extra-virgin olive oil

2 tablespoons red wine vinegar

½ teaspoon honey

½ teaspoon paprika

1 teaspoon sea salt

1 teaspoon freshly ground black pepper

3 mint sprigs, finely chopped

Place the cabbage in a large bowl.

In a small bowl, whisk together the dressing ingredients.

Pour the dressing over the cabbage and gently toss to coat.

Chill in the refrigerator for at least 1 hour before serving.

SALATA SO

WHITE BEAN SALAD

BEL GRAV

Beans grow feverishly in Macedonia. My father's village is particularly known for growing beautiful beans. Growing up, we ate beans regularly in salads, soups and stews. This salad uses white beans, but it can really be made with any bean you like. The addition of mint might sound unusual but it is very common in Macedonian cooking, especially with beans. My parents grow mint in their garden.

2 x 400g tins cannellini beans, rinsed and drained

2 plum tomatoes, seeds removed, diced

1 red pepper, diced

½ medium red onion, finely sliced

DRESSING

2 tablespoons extra-virgin olive oil

Juice of ½ lemon

1 tablespoon coarsely chopped fresh mint, or 1 teaspoon dried mint

¼ teaspoon crushed chilli flakes

½ teaspoon sea salt

Place all of the salad ingredients in a large bowl.

In a small bowl, whisk together the dressing ingredients.

Pour the dressing over the beans and gently toss to coat.

SUPA

Soups

SUPA
Soups

For me, Macedonian soups are the epitome of comfort food.
We grew up eating soups every week, all year round. Many are
hearty, filling and warming for the coldest days of the year; and
some are light and refreshing, like Tarator, a chilled cucumber
soup (page 81) which is served in the hottest months of summer.
Whenever guests would arrive unexpectedly, my grandfather
would jokingly say, "Just add a little broth to the soup and
everyone will have enough." I think about him and smile every
time I make soup.

TARATOR
CHILLED CUCUMBER SOUP

This cold, refreshing soup is very popular in Macedonia during the hot summer months. It is often served with fresh bread and a crisp salad on the side. The flavours are so simple and bright. I've added a bit of cream to round out the tartness of the yogurt and give it a bit of richness.

2 cucumbers, peeled, deseeded and chopped

1 tablespoon sea salt

1 garlic clove, finely minced

1 tablespoon finely chopped fresh dill, plus extra for garnish

1 tablespoon finely chopped fresh mint

1 teaspoon freshly squeezed lemon juice

1 litre plain full-fat Balkan yogurt (or any full-fat yogurt)

120ml double cream

Thinly sliced cucumber, for garnish

Place the cucumbers in a colander and sprinkle with the salt. Set aside to drain for 20 minutes.

In a food processor, combine the cucumbers, garlic, dill, mint and lemon juice. Process for 30 seconds. Scrape down the sides with a spatula and process for another 30 seconds, until you have a thin purée. Transfer to a mixing bowl.

Using a spatula, stir the yogurt and cream into the cucumber mixture.

Refrigerate for at least 2 hours before serving.

When ready to serve, ladle the soup into bowls and garnish with sliced cucumber and dill.

GRAVCHE SUPA

CANNELLINI BEAN SOUP

This is one of my father's specialities and favourite recipes. I can always tell when a pot is on the stove from its comforting aroma, which still brings back fond memories. For periods of religious fasting when meat is prohibited, this soup is made with water instead of chicken stock—a great alternative if you're a vegetarian.

370g dried cannellini beans, soaked for at least 6 hours in plenty of water

2 tablespoons extra-virgin olive oil

1 medium onion, diced

2 carrots, peeled, sliced in half lengthwise and diced

2 garlic cloves, minced

½ teaspoon paprika

¼ teaspoon crushed chilli flakes

500g tinned tomatoes

1 litre low-salt chicken stock

480ml boiling water

2 white potatoes, peeled and cut into 2.5cm pieces

2 teaspoons sea salt

2 teaspoons chopped fresh mint

Freshly ground black pepper

Drain and rinse the beans and place them in a large stockpot. Cover with about 2.5 litres of cold water and bring to a boil over high heat. Reduce the heat to medium-low and simmer for about 1½ hours or until the beans are tender. Drain and set aside.

In a separate large stockpot, heat the oil over medium heat. Add the onion and sauté for 3 to 4 minutes until translucent. Stir in the carrots and continue to cook for 5 or 6 minutes, until tender. Stir in the garlic, paprika and chilli flakes. Sauté for an additional 2 minutes.

Add the tomatoes, chicken stock, boiling water, potatoes and salt. Bring to a boil, and then reduce the heat to medium-low. Stir in the beans and simmer for 30 minutes.

Remove the soup from the heat and stir in the mint and plenty of black pepper.

KIOFTINA SUPA SO
MEATBALL & RICE SOUP WITH SPINACH
ORIZ I SPANAK

This creamy, tart soup is my favourite. It is one of the first dishes I request when I visit my parents, especially in the winter months. I make it often, but it just seems to taste better when my mother makes it. Traditionally, the meatballs are dropped into the broth raw, but I found that roasting them first gives a richer flavour. You can make the meatballs a day ahead.

MEATBALLS

Extra-virgin olive oil, for greasing

450g lean minced beef

1 egg

140g long-grain white rice, rinsed and drained

1 small onion, grated

1 tablespoon chopped parsley

1 tablespoon chopped mint

1 teaspoon sea salt

½ teaspoon ground black pepper

SOUP

1 litre low-salt chicken stock

1 litre cold water

1 tablespoon sea salt

2 eggs

Juice of 1 lemon

60g fresh baby spinach, chopped

Preheat your grill to medium. Lightly grease a baking sheet with olive oil.

In a medium bowl, combine the beef, egg, rice, onion, parsley, mint, salt and pepper. Gently mix until evenly incorporated, but be careful not to overwork the meat. Roll the mixture into balls about 2.5cm in diameter and place them on the baking sheet. Grill the meatballs until just lightly browned, 10 to 12 minutes.

Meanwhile, in a large pot, combine the chicken stock, water and salt. Bring to a simmer over medium heat. Carefully drop the meatballs into the hot stock. Simmer, uncovered, for 25 minutes, skimming off any scum or fat that forms on the surface.

Meanwhile, in a large heat resistant bowl, whisk together the eggs and lemon juice. Whisking constantly, gradually ladle in about a litre of the hot stock from the pot, a little at a time, to temper the eggs.

Remove the soup from the heat. Slowly pour the egg mixture back into the pot and stir in the spinach before serving.

LEKJA SUPA
LENTIL SOUP

This is a warming everyday soup. The addition of tart vinegar at the end adds a bright contrast to the rich and hearty lentils. A splash of vinegar or lemon juice is a common final touch in Macedonian soups. I add a splash more vinegar to my own bowl, and extra chilli flakes for a bit more punch.

300g green lentils

2 tablespoons extra-virgin olive oil

1 medium onion, finely diced

2 carrots, peeled and diced

2 celery stalks, finely diced

4 garlic cloves, minced

¼ teaspoon crushed chilli flakes

1 teaspoon dried oregano

500g tinned tomatoes

1 litre low-salt chicken or vegetable stock

480ml boiling water

1 tablespoon sea salt

1 tablespoon red wine vinegar

Soak the lentils in about 700ml of cold water for 20 minutes. Drain and rinse.

In a large stockpot, heat the olive oil over medium heat. Add the onion and sauté for 3 or 4 minutes until translucent. Add the carrots and celery and sauté until the vegetables are tender, 5 or 6 more minutes. Stir in the garlic, chilli flakes and dried oregano, and continue to cook for an additional 2 minutes.

Pour in the tomatoes, chicken stock, boiling water and salt. Bring to a simmer and stir in the lentils. Simmer, skimming off any scum that forms on the surface, until the lentils are tender but still hold their shape, 35 to 45 minutes.

Remove from the heat and stir in the vinegar before serving.

PILESHKO I ORIZ SUPA SO JATSE I LIMON

CHICKEN & RICE SOUP WITH EGG & LEMON

This warming soup has a creamy lemon broth that is delicious and comforting. The egg thickens the soup without feeling heavy or overly rich. I love it with a dollop of Ajvar (page 27) on top, if you happen to have some.

1 tablespoon extra-virgin olive oil

1 medium onion, finely diced

2 carrots, peeled, diced

2 celery stalks, diced

2–2.25kg whole chicken, loose fat trimmed around the cavity

1 tablespoon sea salt

3 thyme sprigs

3 parsley sprigs, plus extra, chopped, for garnish

2 garlic cloves

1 teaspoon fresh peppercorns

90g long-grain white rice, rinsed and drained

2 eggs

Juice of 1 lemon

In a large pot, heat the oil over medium heat. Sauté the onion until translucent, 4 minutes. Add the carrots and celery and sauté until tender, 5 minutes.

Place the whole chicken on top of the vegetables in the pot. Pour in 2 litres of water and the salt. Using a piece of cheesecloth and kitchen twine, tie the thyme, parsley, garlic and peppercorns into a sealed parcel. Add this to the pot. Bring to a boil, then reduce the heat to medium-low and simmer, uncovered, for 45 minutes, skimming off any scum or fat that forms on the surface. Then remove and discard the herb parcel.

Transfer the chicken to a large clean cutting board and set aside until cool enough to handle. Add the rice to the pot and continue to simmer, uncovered, for 20 minutes, until tender. Meanwhile, carefully remove the chicken meat, discarding the bones and fat. Shred or chop the chicken into bite-size pieces. When the rice is fully cooked, remove the pot from the heat and return the chicken to the soup.

In a large heat resistant bowl, whisk together the eggs and lemon juice. Whisking constantly, gradually ladle in about a litre of the hot stock, a little at a time, to temper the eggs.

Slowly pour the egg mixture back into the soup and stir just to incorporate. Garnish with parsley and serve hot.

BAMJOVA SUPA
SO TELESHKO
MESO

VEAL & OKRA SOUP

My family made this soup when okra was in season in mid- to late summer. My mother loves okra so we had this soup often. Frying the okra before adding it to the soup sears off a bit of the "slime" that occurs naturally, making for a much nicer texture. This is my favourite way to cook with okra because you are just left with its delicate earthy flavour. If you can't find veal, you can easily substitute pork fillet.

30g butter

450g veal fillet,
   cut into 1cm cubes

450g okra, sliced
   diagonally into 6mm pieces

1 medium onion,
   finely diced

2 garlic cloves, minced

1 red pepper, deseeded
   and finely diced

1 carrot, peeled and diced

1 tablespoon tomato purée

1 tablespoon sea salt

¼ teaspoon crushed chilli
   flakes

2 litres boiling water

1 tablespoon coarsely chopped
   fresh parsley, for garnish

Lemon slices, for garnish

In a large stockpot, melt 1 tablespoon of the butter over high heat and sear the veal on all sides, working in batches if necessary. Once the veal is browned, remove the meat from the pot and set it aside.

Reduce the heat to medium and add the remaining tablespoon of butter. Add the okra to the pot and sear on all sides until the "slime" has dissolved, 3 to 4 minutes.

Add the onion, garlic, red pepper and carrot and sauté until the vegetables are tender, 5 to 6 minutes.

Stir in the tomato purée, salt and chilli flakes. Then pour in the boiling water and return the veal to the pot. Simmer for 45 minutes, until the meat is tender.

Garnish with parsley and lemon slices before serving.

ZARZAVAT SUPA

VEGETABLE SOUP

Fresh vegetables are a big deal in Macedonia and in the home gardens of the Macedonian families. This everyday soup is a great way to use whatever vegetables you have on hand, since the quantities can easily be adjusted. It is often made during Lent, when many abstain from eating meat.

1 tablespoon extra-virgin olive oil

1 medium onion, diced

2 carrots, peeled and diced

1 garlic clove, minced

½ teaspoon paprika

500g tinned tomatoes

3 medium white potatoes, peeled and diced

¼ white cabbage, cut into 2.5cm cubes

1 tablespoon sea salt

60g coarsely chopped greens, such as beetroot greens or spinach

1 teaspoon red wine vinegar

2 tablespoons coarsely chopped fresh parsley, for garnish

Freshly ground black pepper

In large stockpot, heat the oil over high heat. Add the onion and sauté until translucent, 3 to 4 minutes. Add the carrots and sauté until tender, 5 to 6 minutes. Stir in the garlic and paprika and cook for an additional 2 minutes.

Pour in the tomatoes and 1.4 litres of water. Add the potatoes, cabbage and salt. Bring to a boil, then reduce the heat to medium and simmer until the vegetables are tender, 20 minutes.

Add the chopped greens and simmer for an additional 5 minutes. Stir in the vinegar and remove from the heat.

Garnish with chopped parsley and black pepper before serving.

SUPA SO ORIZ
I SVINSKO
MESO

PORK & RICE SOUP

My grandparents made this soup for my sister and me whenever they looked after us as children. We were lucky to have them live a few blocks away. I have vivid memories of coming indoors after playing outside on crisp autumn afternoons and finding steaming bowls of this soup ready for us.

450g pork fillet, cut into
   1cm cubes

45g unsalted butter

1 medium onion, diced

1 carrot, peeled and diced

1 green pepper,
   deseeded and diced

½ teaspoon paprika

1 teaspoon dried oregano

½ teaspoon freshly ground
   black pepper

250g tinned tomatoes

1 litre low-salt chicken stock

750ml boiling water

90g long-grain white rice,
   rinsed and drained

Sea salt

Sprinkle the pork with 1 teaspoon of salt.

In a large stockpot, melt the butter over high heat and sear the meat for 5 minutes on each side, or until brown. You may need to work in batches to avoid crowding. Remove the meat from the pot and set aside.

Add the onion to the pot and sauté for 3 to 4 minutes until translucent. Add the carrot and green pepper and sauté until tender, 5 to 6 minutes. Stir in the paprika, oregano, 1 tablespoon of salt and the black pepper.

Add the tomatoes, chicken stock, boiling water and rice. Bring to a boil, then reduce the heat to medium. Return the meat to the pot and simmer for 20 minutes, or until the rice and meat are fully cooked.

RIBENA
FISH SOUP
CHORBA

In Macedonia, especially in the city of Ohrid, fish soup is a celebrated dish, served for several religious holidays. It is also a common remedy for the after-effects of a big night out. When my mother and aunts made this soup, they typically used snapper, but you can use any firm variety of fish you like.

1 tablespoon extra-virgin olive oil, plus extra for drizzling

1 medium onion, thinly sliced

2 carrots, peeled and diced

1 garlic clove, minced

½ teaspoon crushed chilli flakes

1 tablespoon tomato purée

250g tinned tomatoes

4 medium white potatoes, halved lengthwise and cut into 6mm semicircles

1 tablespoon sea salt

900g boneless firm white fish fillets, such as halibut, bass or snapper, sliced into 5cm chunks

1 tablespoon coarsely chopped fresh oregano

Juice of ½ lemon

Freshly ground black pepper

In a large stockpot, heat the olive oil over medium heat. Add the onion and gently sauté for 3 to 4 minutes until translucent. Add the carrots and sauté until tender, 5 to 6 minutes. Stir in the garlic, chilli flakes and tomato purée and cook for an additional 2 minutes.

Pour in the tomatoes and 1.6 litres of water. Add the potatoes and salt. Bring to a boil, then reduce the heat to low and simmer for 15 minutes.

Carefully add the fish and oregano to the pot, and simmer until the potatoes and fish are fully cooked, 5 to 8 minutes.

Stir in the lemon juice. When ready to serve, drizzle with olive oil and top with ground black pepper.

SHKEMBE
TRIPE SOUP
CHORBA

Tripe soup is popular among Macedonians, especially at Easter after midnight mass. My father loved it so my mother made it from time to time. There are many different ways people prepare tripe soup in the different regions of Macedonia but my family makes a lemon and egg broth with fresh dill to balance the richness of the tripe.

540g whole tripe

1 teaspoon extra-virgin
   olive oil

1 large leek (white and light
   green part only), halved
   lengthwise and sliced

90g long-grain white rice,
   rinsed and drained

2 eggs

Juice of 1 lemon

Freshly chopped dill,
   for garnish

Lemon wedges, for serving

Sea salt and freshly ground
   black pepper

Rinse the tripe under cool running water.

In a large stockpot, cover the tripe with about two litres of water and 1 tablespoon of salt. Bring to a boil, then reduce the heat to low. Cover the pot and simmer for 2 hours, until the tripe is very tender.

Drain the tripe and set aside until cool enough to handle, then cut it into 6mm cubes.

Wipe the stockpot dry, and return it to the stovetop. Heat the oil over medium heat and sauté the leek until tender, 3 to 4 minutes. Add the tripe and rice and stir for 1 minute to toast the rice.

Pour in two litres of water and 1 tablespoon of salt. Bring to a boil, then reduce the heat to low and simmer, uncovered, until the rice is cooked, about 20 minutes. Remove from the heat.

In a large heat resistant bowl, whisk together the eggs and lemon juice. Whisking constantly, gradually ladle in about a litre of the hot stock, a little at a time, to temper the eggs. Slowly pour the egg mixture back into the pot and stir to incorporate.

Garnish with the dill and black pepper and serve with lemon wedges.

GRASHEK CHORBA
SPLIT PEA SOUP

This soup is so simple and satisfying. It was one of my father's few go-to recipes. Cinnamon may seem like an unusual addition, but in Macedonian cooking, it is used in both sweet and savoury dishes.

400g dried yellow split peas

2 teaspoons extra-virgin olive oil, plus extra for drizzling

1 medium onion, finely diced

1 teaspoon paprika

2 teaspoons sea salt

1 litre low-salt chicken stock

Cinnamon, for garnish

Rinse the split peas and discard any that are discoloured.

In a large stockpot, heat the olive oil over medium-high heat. Add the onion and sauté until tender, 3 to 4 minutes. Reduce the heat to medium. Add the split peas, paprika and salt, and stir to coat.

Pour in the chicken stock and a litre of water. Cover and simmer gently for 1½ to 2 hours until the peas are soft.

Remove from the heat and let cool. When ready to serve, return the soup to the pot and heat through. Garnish with a drizzle of olive oil and a light sprinkle of cinnamon.

MESO

Meats

MESO
Meats

When my parents were growing up in Macedonia, meat was a luxury reserved only for celebrations and special occasions. Day-to-day meals in the villages were made up of an array of vegetables, beans and legumes. Even for my father's family, who were shepherds, lamb was only served a few times a year, for Easter, name days or weddings. The costly meat would be reserved to sell, and the family often couldn't afford the indulgence.

Pork was also customary during celebrations throughout the year, especially at weddings, where a whole roast suckling pig played a symbolic role in the celebration, during the bieshetoe oro (pig dance, see page 16). Beef was a rarer luxury; the region my parents come from is mountainous, without the rolling fields needed to raise cattle.

When an animal was slaughtered, every part would be utilised. Stews and braises use low and slow cooking techniques in order to break down tougher cuts of meat, and more tender cuts are typically grilled or pan-fried. Any unused meat was submerged in lard and stored in clay pots to preserve it for the colder months.

Today, meat has become much more common in day-to-day meals because of the convenience of grocery stores and refrigeration. However, respect for the animal is ingrained in the culture, and meat is almost always served with some fanfare as the centrepiece of the meal.

ZELKOVA
CABBAGE STEW
MANGIA

This is a classic, hearty Macedonian stew. White cabbage grows abundantly in Macedonia and is very popular in Macedonian cooking. This is one of my father's go-to recipes and we love his slightly spicy broth. My family makes this stew all year round but it is especially good in the winter. I like to crumble a bit of feta cheese over the top—the feta almost melts into the broth.

900g boneless pork shoulder, fat trimmed, cut into 2.5cm cubes

1 tablespoon extra-virgin olive oil

1 medium onion, diced

½ hot banana pepper, deseeded and finely diced, or ½ teaspoon crushed chilli flakes

2 garlic cloves, minced

1 teaspoon freshly ground black pepper

1 teaspoon paprika

240ml red wine

250g tinned tomatoes

1 litre boiling water

1 medium white cabbage, cored, chopped into 1cm pieces

Crumbled feta cheese, for serving (optional)

Sea salt

Pat the pork dry using paper towels and sprinkle the meat with 1 teaspoon of salt.

In a large stockpot, heat the oil over high heat and sear the pork for 3 or 4 minutes per side until golden brown (you may need to work in batches to avoid crowding the pot). Remove and set aside.

Drain all but about 1 teaspoon of fat from the pot. Reduce the heat to medium. Add the onion and banana pepper or chilli flakes and sauté for 3 to 4 minutes until tender. Stir in the garlic, 1 tablespoon salt, the black pepper and paprika. Sauté for an additional 2 minutes.

Pour in the red wine and simmer for 4 to 5 minutes to reduce the liquid by half. Pour in the tomatoes and boiling water. Return the pork to the pot. Reduce the heat to low and simmer, covered, for 2 hours.

Remove the lid and add the cabbage. Stir just to submerge the cabbage in the liquid and simmer, uncovered, for an additional 40 minutes, until the pork is tender.

Serve with crumbled feta, if desired.

JAGNESHKA
MANGIA SO
PRAZ I KOMPIRI

LAMB, LEEK & POTATO STEW

My grandfather was a self-taught chef and had a thriving restaurant in Toronto. He would make this stew for us whenever we visited for Sunday lunch. In the villages where my grandparents grew up, this stew would typically be made in the spring, in the months after Easter while lamb was readily available. I love making this for a small group of friends or family coming over because it can be made in advance and reheated without compromising the flavour of the stew.

450g boneless leg of lamb, fat trimmed, cut into 2.5cm cubes
2 tablespoons extra-virgin olive oil
4 leeks, cut into 1cm rings (white and light green parts only)
½ hot banana pepper, finely diced, or ½ teaspoon crushed chilli flakes
2 garlic cloves, thinly sliced
1 tablespoon plain flour
700ml boiling water
2 tablespoons tomato purée
4–6 large white potatoes, sliced into wedges
1 teaspoon ground black pepper
1 tablespoon coarsely chopped fresh mint, for serving
Sea salt

Preheat the oven to 180°C. Sprinkle the lamb with 1 teaspoon of salt.

In a Dutch oven or large sauté pan, heat the oil over high heat and sear the lamb for 3 to 4 minutes per side, until golden brown (you may need to work in batches to avoid crowding the pot). Remove and set aside.

Reduce the heat to medium. Add the leeks and hot pepper or chilli flakes and sauté for 3 to 4 minutes until tender. Stir in the garlic and flour. Sauté for an additional 2 minutes.

Pour in the boiling water. Add the tomato purée, potatoes, lamb and 1 tablespoon of sea salt. If using a sauté pan, carefully transfer the ingredients to a baking dish.

Cover with a lid or foil and bake in the oven for 1 hour. Uncover and bake for an additional 15 minutes.

Just before serving, garnish with black pepper and fresh mint.

KREMENADLI
GRILLED PORK CHOPS

These mildly spiced pork chops pair well with nearly any salad or side dish in this book. Using a mortar and pestle to create the paste really brings the flavours together, and is worth the extra effort.

2 garlic cloves, coarsely chopped
3 tablespoons extra-virgin olive oil
1 teaspoon paprika
1 tablespoon sea salt
2 teaspoons freshly ground black pepper
4 thick-cut, bone-in pork chops (about 1.4kg in total)

Using a mortar and pestle, mash the garlic with the oil, paprika, salt and black pepper to form a paste.

Pat the pork chops dry using paper towels. Smear the paste all over the meat. Transfer to a dish and cover with a lid or cling film. Refrigerate for at least 1 hour to marinate.

Preheat a grill or a cast iron skillet to high heat. Sear the pork chops for 4 to 6 minutes on each side until golden brown and just cooked through.

Remove the pork chops from the heat and let them rest for 5 minutes before serving.

POLNETI
STUFFED PEPPERS
PIPERKI

This is such a popular dish in Macedonian cooking. Everyone has a different take, but traditionally the stuffing is made with minced beef and rice. Depending on what looks best at the butcher, I sometimes substitute other minced meats as well, particularly pork. My Aunt Sophie used to make the best stuffed peppers in our family and her tip was to put tomato slices on top to keep the rice moist while baking.

8 large peppers, 6mm cut off
the tops, seeds removed

Olive oil

450g lean minced beef

2 medium onions, grated

180g long-grain white
rice, rinsed and drained

4 garlic cloves, minced

1½ teaspoons sea salt

1 teaspoon freshly ground
black pepper

1 tablespoon dried oregano

1 teaspoon paprika

2 teaspoons tomato purée

1 cup red wine

12g fresh parsley, finely
chopped

Boiling water

2 large tomatoes, cut into
8 thick slices

Preheat the oven to 180°C. In a deep baking dish or Dutch oven, arrange the peppers upright so that they fit snugly and won't topple over.

In a large sauté pan, heat 1 teaspoon of olive oil over high heat. Add the minced beef and cook, stirring constantly, until the meat is just cooked. Drain the fat from the meat and set the meat aside.

In the same pan, heat 2 tablespoons of olive oil over medium heat. Add the onions, rice, garlic, salt, black pepper, oregano, paprika and tomato purée. Sauté, stirring, for 1 minute, just to toast the rice. Pour in the wine and bring to a simmer. Remove the pan from the heat and stir in the meat, parsley and 240ml of boiling water.

Loosely fill each pepper with the meat and rice mixture to just below the brim of the pepper. Gently press one slice of tomato on top of the opening of each pepper.

Pour 120ml of boiling water into the bottom of the baking dish. Tightly cover the dish with a lid or foil and bake for 30 minutes.

Remove the lid or foil and bake for an additional 30 minutes, until the peppers are tender and the rice is cooked.

SVINSKI REBRA SO GRAVCHE

PORK RIB & BUTTER BEAN STEW

This was one of my grandfather's specialities, and no one could make it quite as well as he could. The memory of him and my nostalgia for this dish is why it is one of my favourite recipes.

550g large dried butter beans, soaked for at least 6 hours in plenty of water, drained

60ml olive oil

900g pork spareribs, sliced between the bones

2 medium onions, diced

2 carrots, peeled and diced

2 celery stalks, diced

2 tablespoons tomato purée

2 garlic cloves, sliced

¼ teaspoon crushed chilli flakes

1 teaspoon dried oregano

2 litres boiling water

1 tablespoon coarsely chopped fresh mint, for garnish

Sea salt

Place the beans in a large pot and cover with cold water. Bring to a boil, then reduce the heat to low and simmer for 1 hour. Drain and set aside.

Preheat the oven to 180°C. In a large roasting pan placed over 2 burners (or in a large frying pan over 1 burner), heat the olive oil over high heat. Sprinkle the ribs with 1 teaspoon of salt. Sear the ribs until golden brown on all sides (you may need to do this in batches). Remove and set aside.

Reduce the heat to medium and, in the same pan, sauté the onions, carrots and celery until tender, 8 to 10 minutes. Stir in the tomato purée, garlic, chilli flakes, oregano and 1 teaspoon of salt. Sauté for an additional 2 minutes. If using a large frying pan, transfer the vegetables to a large roasting pan or baking dish.

Gently stir the beans into the vegetables. Nestle the ribs into the mixture. Pour in just enough of the boiling water to cover the beans, and sprinkle with 1 tablespoon of salt. Use a wooden spoon or spatula to push the ribs and beans down so they are submerged in the liquid. Cover the roasting pan or dish with a lid or foil and bake in the oven for 30 minutes. Remove the lid or foil and bake, uncovered, for an additional 45 minutes to 1 hour, until the beans are fully cooked and the ribs are tender.

Garnish with fresh mint before serving.

MUSAKA SO
MESO, KOMPIRI
I PATLIJANI

LAMB, AUBERGINE & POTATO CASSEROLE

Typically, this is a very rich dish but I've taken a slightly lighter approach with my recipe. The traditional way to make this dish is to fry the aubergine and potatoes before putting it all together, which is delicious but very heavy. I prefer to roast the aubergine slices and boil the potatoes before assembly, and everyone I've made this for loves it just as much.

3 medium aubergines, peeled and sliced into 1cm thick rounds

4 tablespoons extra-virgin olive oil, plus extra for greasing

4 large white potatoes, peeled and sliced into 1cm thick rounds

450g lean minced lamb

1 large onion, finely diced

1 green pepper, seeds removed, finely diced

2 garlic cloves, minced

¼ teaspoon crushed chilli flakes

½ teaspoon freshly ground black pepper

Preheat the oven to 190°C. Grease a 30 x 40cm baking dish and a large baking sheet with olive oil.

Brush both sides of the aubergine slices with 3 tablespoons of the olive oil and sprinkle with 1 teaspoon of salt. Arrange the aubergine slices on the baking sheet in a single layer (in batches if necessary). Bake for 15 minutes until just slightly golden brown. Flip the aubergine slices and bake for an additional 15 minutes. Remove and set aside.

Place the potatoes in a large stockpot, fill with water to cover, and add 1 tablespoon of salt. Bring to a boil, then reduce the heat to medium and simmer for 5 minutes. Drain the potatoes well and lay them out on a tray lined with paper towels to dry as much as possible.

In a large sauté pan, heat the remaining tablespoon of olive oil over high heat. Add the lamb and cook, stirring constantly, until the meat is just cooked through. Remove the lamb and set aside. Drain all but about 1 tablespoon of fat from the pan.

Continued

120ml red wine

2 medium tomatoes,
   peeled and diced

125g tinned tomatoes

150g grated Parmesan cheese

Sea salt

SAUCE

115g unsalted butter

60g plain flour

1 litre whole milk, warmed

½ teaspoon nutmeg

1 teaspoon sea salt

3 egg yolks

Reduce the heat to medium. In the same pan, sauté the onion and green pepper for 3 to 4 minutes until tender. Stir in the garlic, chilli flakes, 1 teaspoon of salt and the black pepper. Sauté for an additional 2 minutes.

Pour in the red wine and bring to a simmer. Stir in the diced tomatoes, tinned tomatoes and lamb. Remove from the heat and set aside.

Arrange the sliced potatoes on the bottom of the greased baking dish, overlapping them slightly. Spoon half of the lamb mixture on top and spread evenly over the potatoes. Now layer the aubergine slices on top of the meat, overlapping them slightly. Spread the remaining meat mixture over the aubergines, and sprinkle with 50g of the Parmesan cheese. Set aside.

To make the sauce, melt the butter in a medium stockpot and whisk in the flour. Continue to whisk for 2 minutes until a roux forms. Whisk in the milk and continue to whisk for about 5 minutes until the sauce is free of lumps and begins to thicken. Mix in the nutmeg and salt and remove from the heat.

In a medium heatproof bowl, whisk the egg yolks. Whisking continuously, slowly ladle about 250ml of the hot sauce into the egg yolks to temper them. Pour the egg mixture into the sauce and stir to incorporate. Ladle the sauce on top of the casserole.

Sprinkle the dish with the remaining 100g of Parmesan cheese and bake, uncovered, for 45 to 55 minutes, or until golden brown.

SARMI OD ZELKA

CABBAGE ROLLS

This classic Macedonian dish is made often and is an important part of the traditional Christmas Eve meal, when immediate family enjoy a "lean meal" as part of the religious tradition. On Christmas Eve, Sarmi are traditionally served along with Tavche Gravche *(Traditional White Bean Stew, page 177),* Pitulitsi *(Fritters, page 238), boiled potatoes and fruit.*

1 whole green cabbage,
   stem and core removed
4 rashers of streaky bacon,
   diced
225g lean minced pork
½ medium onion,
   finely diced
1 celery stalk, finely diced
1½ tablespoons tomato purée
1 teaspoon dried oregano
90g long-grain white rice,
   rinsed and drained
120ml boiling water
1 teaspoon red wine vinegar
1 egg, beaten
Olive oil, for greasing
240ml tomato sauce
Sea salt

Fill a large stockpot with water and add 1 tablespoon of salt. Submerge the whole cabbage in the water. Bring to a boil, then reduce the heat and simmer until the leaves are tender, 20 to 30 minutes. Drain the cabbage and set aside until just cool enough to handle. Carefully peel away one leaf at a time being careful not to tear them. Place leaves flat on a towel to dry. They must be opaque and pliable.

To make the filling, heat a large sauté pan over medium-high heat and cook the bacon until slightly crispy, about 5 minutes. Remove and set aside.

In the same pan, cook the minced pork, stirring constantly, until the meat is just cooked through. Drain the fat and set the meat aside.

Add the onion and celery and sauté for 3 to 4 minutes until tender. Return the bacon and minced pork to the pan and add the tomato purée, oregano, and 1½ teaspoons of salt. Add the rice and sauté for 1 minute until just toasted. Pour in the boiling water and vinegar and remove from the heat. Let the mixture cool for 10 minutes, and then stir in the egg.

Preheat the oven to 180°C. Grease a 23 by 33cm baking dish with olive oil. Using a paring knife, slice off the raised part of the large vein at the base of one cabbage leaf so that it is flush with the rest of the leaf. Lay the leaf flat and place a heaping spoonful of the filling just above the base. Carefully roll the base over the filling and tuck in the sides of the leaf. Continue to roll up until you have a tight parcel. Repeat with the rest of the leaves and filling, carefully placing the cabbage rolls in the baking dish, seam side down, so that they fit snugly in a single layer. Pour the tomato sauce over the rolls.

Cover the baking dish with a lid or foil and bake for 45 minutes. Remove the lid and bake, uncovered, for an additional 15 minutes. Check to make sure the rice is cooked through before serving.

GOVEDSKO
MESO SO
KROMIT

BEEF & ONION STEW

This recipe is really simple to put together, but make sure you allow enough time for the stew to braise. Slow braising is the secret to really tender beef. This recipe is great in spring when green onions are in season, but pearl onions work just fine.

900g chuck steak, cut into 2.5cm pieces

2 teaspoons sea salt

1 tablespoon extra-virgin olive oil

2 carrots, peeled and diced

2 garlic cloves, minced

1 tomato, diced

¼ teaspoon crushed chilli flakes

1 teaspoon dried oregano

¼ teaspoon cinnamon

1 tablespoon flour

240ml red wine

480ml boiling water

½ teaspoon freshly ground black pepper

400g peeled young baby onions, cipollini or pearl onions (frozen ok)

Preheat the oven to 150°C.

Pat the beef dry with paper towels and sprinkle the meat with 1 teaspoon of the salt.

In a Dutch oven, heat the oil over high heat. Sear the meat for 3 to 4 minutes on each side until browned. You may need to work in batches to avoid crowding the pot. If working in batches, return the meat to the pot.

Add the carrots, garlic, tomato, chilli flakes, oregano and cinnamon and sauté for 3 to 4 minutes until the carrots begin to soften.

Sprinkle the flour over the meat and vegetables in the pot and stir until the meat looks dry and pasty. Pour in the wine. Reduce the heat to medium and simmer until the wine reduces by half, 4 to 5 minutes.

Pour in the boiling water and add the remaining teaspoon of salt and the black pepper. Stir in the onions, cover with a lid or foil, and braise in the oven for 2½ hours. Remove the lid and bake, uncovered, for an additional 20 minutes.

TURLI TAVA
MEAT STEW WITH VEGETABLES
SO MESO

Combining different meats in one recipe is actually quite common in Macedonian cuisine. This is a very traditional recipe that I learned from my grandfather. It is perhaps a nod to a time when people used whatever was available. There is something really rustic and ancient about this meal that I love, since I know as it has been passed down through generations.

30g unsalted butter

225g lean stewing beef, cut into 2.5cm chunks

225g pork shoulder, cut into 2.5cm chunks

225g stewing veal, cut into 2.5cm chunks

1 medium onion, grated

2 garlic cloves, minced

1 teaspoon paprika

1 teaspoon dried oregano

240ml red wine

500g tinned tomatoes

240ml boiling water

2 medium white potatoes, peeled and diced

450g fresh green beans, trimmed

4-6 oregano sprigs, for garnish

Sea salt

Preheat the oven to 150°C.

In a large Dutch oven, melt the butter over high heat. Sprinkle all of the meats with 2 teaspoons of salt and sear for 3 to 4 minutes on each side until golden brown (you may need to work in batches). Remove the meat and set aside.

Reduce the heat to medium. Add the onion to the pot and sauté for 2 minutes. Stir in the garlic, paprika and dried oregano and sauté for an additional 2 minutes.

Pour in the wine and simmer for 4 to 5 minutes, until reduced by half. Add the tomatoes, boiling water, 1 tablespoon of salt and the meat. Stir to combine and bring to a simmer.

Cover with a lid or foil and bake for 2½ hours. Remove the lid and stir in the potatoes and green beans. Bake, uncovered, for an additional hour, or until the potatoes are cooked and the beans are tender.

Garnish with fresh oregano before serving.

PECHENA NOGA OD JAGNE

ROASTED LEG OF LAMB

Easter is one of the most important celebrations in Macedonia. It is common for each family to roast a whole lamb on a spit. My family did this every year and it was an incredible tradition to grow up with. Spit-roasting lamb is a very involved process and actually not one that I am really skilled at. This recipe is great for smaller gatherings and an easier way to enjoy lamb. I make it for Easter but you could make it for any special occasion.

2–2.25kg whole bone-in leg
of lamb

2 teaspoons freshly ground
black pepper

2 tablespoons extra-virgin
olive oil

4 medium white potatoes,
peeled and cut into wedges

3 medium tomatoes,
cut into wedges

3 garlic cloves, minced

2 tablespoons chopped
fresh mint

1 tablespoon chopped
fresh parsley

Juice of 1 lemon

Sea salt

Preheat the oven to 150°C. Let the lamb sit at room temperature for 15 minutes. Pat dry with a paper towel and, using a sharp knife, score the fat in a cross-hatch pattern. Rub the lamb with 1 tablespoon of salt and the black pepper.

Heat a large Dutch oven over high heat for 3 to 4 minutes. Pour in the oil and carefully place the lamb in the pot. Sear for about 5 to 6 minutes per side. Add about 240ml of water to the pot. Cover with a lid or foil and roast in the oven for 4 hours.

In a bowl, toss together the potatoes, tomatoes, garlic, mint, parsley and 1 teaspoon of salt.

Remove the meat from the oven and scatter the potatoes and tomatoes around the base of the meat. Return to the oven and roast, uncovered, for an additional 40 to 45 minutes until the potatoes are cooked through.

Remove from the oven and pour the lemon juice over the lamb and vegetables. Let the meat rest for 10 minutes before serving.

SVINSKO PECHENO SO KISELA

ROASTED PORK WITH SAUERKRAUT & RICE

ZELKA I ORIZ

My grandfather made his own sauerkraut that tasted amazing, but I also love a good quality shop-bought sauerkraut. This dish looks really sophisticated, but it is quite easy to make. Sometimes I make it with bone-in pork chops instead of pork loin.

15g unsalted butter

900g pork loin

5 rashers of streaky bacon, diced

½ medium onion, diced

1 teaspoon paprika

½ teaspoon freshly ground black pepper

180g long-grain white rice, rinsed and drained

420g sauerkraut, rinsed and drained

830ml boiling water

½ teaspoon finely chopped dill

Sea salt

Preheat the oven to 190°C. In a large Dutch oven, melt the butter over high heat. Sprinkle the pork with ½ teaspoon of sea salt and sear for 4 to 5 minutes on each side until golden brown. Remove and set aside.

Reduce the heat to medium. Add the bacon and cook for 3 to 4 minutes, stirring occasionally, until the fat renders. Remove the bacon and set it aside. Drain all but about 1 teaspoon of the fat left in the pot. Add the onion to the pot and sauté for 3 to 4 minutes until tender. Sprinkle in the paprika, 1 teaspoon of salt and the black pepper. Stir in the rice and bacon and stir for 1 minute to toast the rice. Add the sauerkraut and boiling water, making sure that the rice is fully submerged in water.

Nestle the pork loin on top of the sauerkraut and rice. Cover with a lid or foil and bake for 20 to 25 minutes until the rice is cooked.

Remove the pork loin from the pot and set aside to rest for 5 minutes. Gently fold the dill into the rice mixture. Slice the pork diagonally, against the grain of the meat, and serve with the rice and sauerkraut.

PASTRMAJLIJA
MEAT PIE

The word pastrma *means salted dried meat. Pastrmajlija is Macedonia's much-loved version of pizza and it can be found in restaurants, markets and cafes throughout the region. In parts of Macedonia there are festivals devoted solely to this dish. It is a popular late-night meal after a night of dancing.*

MACEDONIA

128

DOUGH

350ml warm water
7g fast action dried yeast
½ teaspoon sugar
500g plain flour, sifted, plus
    extra for dusting
1 tablespoon sea salt
2 tablespoons extra-virgin olive
    oil, plus extra for greasing

FILLING

450g pork loin, cut into 1cm
    chunks
70g butter, melted
1 tablespoon extra-virgin
    olive oil
2 teaspoons sea salt
½ teaspoon paprika
3 eggs, beaten

To make the dough, place the warm water in a small bowl. Add the yeast and sugar. Cover the bowl with a plate and let stand until the yeast begins to foam, about 10 minutes.

In a large bowl, whisk together the flour and salt. Make a well in the centre. Pour the yeast mixture and the oil into the well. Using a spatula, gently fold the flour into the liquid until incorporated and a dough begins to form. Transfer the dough to a lightly floured work surface and knead until smooth and elastic, about 10 minutes. Lightly dust the surface of the dough with flour if it feels sticky. Lightly grease a large bowl with a thin layer of olive oil and place the dough inside. Brush the top of the dough with a thin layer of olive oil. Cover the bowl with a large plate and set aside in a warm place to rise for 1 hour.

Meanwhile, toss together the pork, melted butter, olive oil, salt and paprika. Refrigerate for 1 hour to marinate.

Preheat the oven to 180°C. Grease a 53 by 38cm baking sheet with olive oil.

Place the dough on a clean work surface. Roll the dough into a rectangle 6mm thick, and about 5cm larger than your baking sheet. Carefully transfer the dough to the baking sheet. Fold the edges of the dough over to create a border. Spread the meat over the dough in a single layer. Brush the edges of the dough with a little of the beaten eggs and set the remainder aside.

Bake the pie for 20 minutes. Remove from the oven and pour the remaining eggs over the meat. Return to the oven and bake for an additional 7 to 10 minutes, until the eggs are cooked and the dough is golden brown.

ZHIVINA

Poultry

ZHIVINA
Poultry

Poultry is a widely used ingredient in Macedonian cooking. In my parents' villages, chickens would roam the gardens and were a natural part of the agricultural landscape. Macedonia also has a wide selection of game birds that are sometimes used in similar recipes. Growing up, I remember travelling through the villages of Macedonia with my parents, eating at relatives' homes or in local restaurants, and the chicken dishes were among the best I've ever had. All of the recipes in this chapter are common throughout the regions of Macedonia and are simple, rustic and full of flavour.

ZACHINETO
PILESHKO

SPICED CHICKEN

This dish, traditionally roasted in a furna (a wood-fired oven), is one of the best dishes you can have in Macedonia. The chicken is typically roasted in a shallow, glazed clay casserole and served with fresh bread.

3 tablespoons extra-virgin
   olive oil

2 teaspoons sea salt

1 teaspoon paprika

½ teaspoon cinnamon

¼ teaspoon cayenne pepper

1.5–2kg whole chicken, jointed

2 medium onions,
   cut into wedges

4–6 whole garlic cloves, peeled

In a large bowl, whisk together the oil, salt, paprika, cinnamon and cayenne to make a marinade.

Place the chicken, onions and garlic in a large bowl. Pour over the marinade and toss by hand. Make sure all of the pieces are evenly coated. Cover with cling film and refrigerate for 1 hour to marinate.

Preheat the oven to 200°C.

Arrange the onions and garlic on the bottom of a 23 by 33cm baking dish (or a clay casserole if you have one). Place the chicken pieces (skin side up) on top of the onions. Roast, uncovered, for 30 to 35 minutes, until the chicken is fully cooked.

Put under a hot grill for 3 to 4 minutes, watching carefully, to crisp up the chicken skin.

TAVA SO PILESHKI GRADI

FRIED CHICKEN BREASTS

Whenever my sister and I would sleep over at my cousin's house, my aunt would make these for us. She was an incredible cook. They make great sandwiches, tucked into Poupchina (Bread Rolls, page 215) with fresh lettuce and Ajvar (Roasted Red Pepper and Aubergine Dip, page 27).

4 boneless skinless
　chicken breasts
125g plain flour
3 eggs, beaten
115g dried breadcrumbs
2 teaspoons paprika
1 teaspoon freshly ground
　black pepper
60ml vegetable oil, for frying
Sea salt

SAUCE

Juice of 1 lemon
Zest of ½ lemon
12g parsley, chopped

First make the sauce. In a small bowl, whisk together the lemon juice, lemon zest and parsley. Set aside.

One at a time, place the chicken breasts in a large zip-top plastic bag or between two pieces of cling film or parchment paper. Pound out using a meat mallet until each breast is about 1cm thick.

In a shallow dish, whisk the flour together with 1½ teaspoons of salt. Place the eggs in a second shallow dish. In a third shallow dish, whisk together the breadcrumbs, paprika, 1½ teaspoons of salt and the black pepper.

Coat each chicken breast in the seasoned flour and shake off excess. Then coat each breast with beaten eggs and shake off excess. Finally, place each breast in the breadcrumbs, making sure each piece is evenly coated.

In a large sauté pan, heat the oil until it begins to shimmer. Carefully place the coated chicken breasts into the hot oil (working in batches if necessary). Fry for 3 to 4 minutes on each side, until golden brown and cooked through. Transfer the cooked chicken to a plate lined with paper towels to drain excess oil.

Place on a plate and spoon over the lemon and parsley sauce before serving.

PILESHKI
CHICKEN SKEWERS
RAZHNITSI

One of the best cooking secrets my grandfather taught me was to marinate chicken breasts in yogurt. The enzymes in the yogurt tenderise the meat. These skewers are common street food in Macedonia and we often had them at family barbecues. You will need 8 to 10 metal or pre-soaked bamboo skewers (soak for 20 minutes).

900g boneless skinless chicken thighs, cut into 2.5cm cubes

350ml plain full-fat Balkan yogurt (or any full-fat yogurt)

1 teaspoon sea salt

1 tablespoon extra-virgin olive oil

1 tablespoon chopped fresh mint, plus extra to garnish

In a large bowl, combine the chicken, yogurt, salt, olive oil and mint. Mix to coat. Cover and refrigerate for at least 2 hours and up to 24 hours to marinate.

Skewer 2 to 3 pieces of chicken towards the top end of each skewer.

Heat a grill pan or grill to medium-high heat. Grill the chicken skewers for 4 to 5 minutes on each side until golden brown and fully cooked.

Garnish with the remaining mint before serving.

PILINJA PECHENI

BRAISED QUAIL

Game birds are quite popular in Macedonia. They can be found in the lowlands and open fields, particularly in the regions of Pelegonjia and Dolnesko. If you can't find quails in your local market, you can easily substitute Cornish hens or chicken thighs in this recipe; just adjust the cooking time accordingly. Serve this dish with Pilav Od Oriz (Rice Pilaf, page 181) or Pecheni Kompiri (Roasted Potatoes, page 178).

4 quail, backbone removed, spatchcocked

30g butter, at room temperature

½ teaspoon sea salt

¼ teaspoon paprika

¼ teaspoon nutmeg

240ml red wine

240ml small peeled pearl onions (frozen are fine)

Chopped parsley, for garnish

Preheat the oven to 200°C.

In a small dish, mix together the butter, salt, paprika and nutmeg. Smear the butter mixture all over the quail.

Heat an oven-proof frying pan, preferably cast iron, over high heat and brown the quail for 2 to 3 minutes on each side, just until the skin turns golden brown. Remove the quail and set aside.

Reduce the heat to medium. Pour the wine into the skillet. Add the onions and simmer until the wine has reduced by half, 4 to 5 minutes.

Return the quail to the skillet and roast in the oven until just cooked through, 10 to 12 minutes.

Sprinkle with chopped parsley and serve immediately.

GERSHLASO PILESHKO MESO

CHICKEN & ORZO

Once you try it, this recipe is sure to become one of your favourites. My mother made this often for weeknight meals and to serve to guests. It has now become one of my favourites for entertaining. Whenever I make this for friends who haven't tried it, they always request it when they come over again.

8 boneless skinless
  chicken thighs
30g unsalted butter
1 teaspoon extra-virgin olive oil
1 medium onion, finely diced
2 garlic cloves, minced
¼ teaspoon crushed chilli
  flakes
¼ teaspoon nutmeg
¼ teaspoon cinnamon
240ml red wine
1 tablespoon tomato purée
300ml hot water
2 teaspoons sea salt
225g dried orzo

Preheat the oven to 180°C. Pat the chicken dry using paper towels.

In a Dutch oven, melt the butter with the oil over medium-high heat. Add the chicken thighs (top side down) and sear on one side only for 3 to 4 minutes until golden brown. Remove the chicken and set aside.

Reduce the heat to medium. Add the onion to the pot and sauté for 3 to 4 minutes until tender. Stir in the garlic, chilli flakes, nutmeg and cinnamon, and sauté for an additional 2 minutes.

Pour in the red wine and simmer until it has reduced by half, 4 to 5 minutes. Stir in the tomato purée, hot water and salt.

Pour in the orzo and spread it evenly over the bottom of the pot. Gently nestle the chicken (browned side up) into the orzo. Bring the liquid to a simmer.

Remove from the heat, cover with a lid or foil, and bake in the oven for 20 to 25 minutes until the orzo and chicken are cooked through.

PILESHKI

CHICKEN PIE

MUSAKA

My sister calls this "the recipe to make when you're not sure what to make". It is so easy to put together and makes great leftovers. The sour cream really adds another dimension of flavour and richness to the chicken. It is one of our favourite comfort-food dishes.

900g boneless skinless chicken breasts, cut into 2.5cm cubes

1 teaspoon finely chopped fresh oregano

1 teaspoon finely chopped fresh thyme

30g unsalted butter

1 medium onion, diced

220g plus 1 tablespoon plain flour

½ teaspoon freshly ground black pepper

125ml whole milk

5 eggs, beaten

480ml sour cream

1 tablespoon extra-virgin olive oil, plus extra for greasing

Sea salt

Preheat the oven to 190°C. Grease a 23 by 33cm baking dish with olive oil.

In a large bowl, combine the chicken, oregano, thyme and 1 teaspoon of salt.

In a small sauté pan, melt the butter over medium heat. Add the onion and sauté for 3 to 4 minutes until tender. Pour the onion and butter into the bowl with the chicken. Toss to coat and set aside.

In a separate bowl, whisk together 220g of flour, 2 teaspoons salt and the black pepper, milk and eggs until you have a smooth batter.

Pour the batter into the oiled baking dish to create a base. Scatter the chicken and onion mixture over the batter in a single layer.

Bake for 30 minutes until golden brown and cooked through. Remove from the oven and turn on your grill.

Mix together the sour cream, olive oil and the remaining flour. Spoon the sour cream mixture over the chicken and grill for about 5 minutes until the top is golden brown and bubbling.

PILESHKI PILAV

CHICKEN & RICE

We have a running joke in our family about my mother's devoted love of chicken and rice. There is something really homey about taking a large tepsi (roasting pan) out of the oven and setting it on the table with the people you love around you. This dish is usually served with a selection of salads and Kisolo Mleko So Pechen Luk (Yogurt with Garlic, Cucumber and Dill, page 31).

1.5–2kg whole chicken, jointed

½ teaspoon paprika

30g unsalted butter

1 large leek (white and light green part only), halved lengthwise and sliced

1 garlic clove, minced

¼ teaspoon crushed chilli flakes

1 tablespoon tomato purée

280g long-grain white rice

700ml boiling water

3–4 oregano sprigs

Sea salt

Preheat the oven to 180°C.

Sprinkle the chicken pieces with 1 teaspoon salt and the paprika.

In a large Dutch oven, melt the butter over medium-high heat. Place the chicken (skin side down) into the hot butter and sear on one side only until the skin is golden brown, 5 to 7 minutes. Remove and set aside. Save about 1 tablespoon of fat in the pot and discard the excess.

Reduce the heat to medium. Add the leek and sauté until tender, 3 to 4 minutes. Stir in the garlic, 1 teaspoon salt and the crushed chilli flakes. Sauté for an additional 2 minutes.

Add the tomato purée and rice and stir for about 1 minute to toast the rice.

Pour in the boiling water and gently nestle the chicken pieces (skin side up) into the rice. Place the oregano sprigs on top.

Cover with a lid or foil and bake for 25 minutes or until the chicken and rice are fully cooked.

PILESHKO POLNETO SO PRAZI

STUFFED CHICKEN WITH LEEKS & CHEESE

SIRENJE

This dish looks so fancy and sophisticated but it is really quite easy to make. Leeks, feta and ricotta is a common filling in Macedonian dishes, and the combination is delicious. The sweetness of the leeks is a perfect balance to the salty creaminess of the cheese. Toothpicks help to hold the chicken together in the oven. If you can't find skin-on boneless chicken breasts, ask your butcher to prepare them for you.

MACEDONIA

148

4 skin-on boneless chicken
  breasts
½ teaspoon sea salt
¼ teaspoon paprika
15g unsalted butter
1 teaspoon vegetable oil

FILLING

2 large leeks (white and light
  green parts only), diced
15g unsalted butter
1½ teaspoons sea salt
¼ teaspoon paprika
1 teaspoon fresh thyme
60g ricotta cheese
40g grated feta cheese

Preheat the oven to 200°C. Line a baking sheet with parchment paper. Carefully slice the chicken halfway through the breast to create a pocket.

Make the filling: In a large sauté pan, melt the butter over medium heat. Add the leeks, salt, paprika and thyme. Sauté until tender, 3 to 4 minutes. Meanwhile, in a medium bowl, mix the ricotta and feta. Once the leeks are cooked, fold them into the cheese mixture and set aside.

Stuff each chicken breast pocket with a heaped spoonful of filling. Use a toothpick to seal the openings. Season on both sides with the salt and paprika.

In a large sauté pan, melt the butter over high heat and add the vegetable oil. Place the chicken breasts (skin side down) into the pan and sear for 3 to 4 minutes until golden brown. Then flip and sear the other side for 3 to 4 minutes.

Transfer the breasts to the baking sheet (skin side up) and roast for 10 to 12 minutes until fully cooked. Carefully remove the toothpicks just before serving.

PECHENA KOKOSHKA SO ZELKA I KOMPIRI

ROASTED CORNISH HENS WITH CABBAGE & POTATOES

I love the delicate flavour of Cornish hens with wilted cabbage.
This recipe is so simple and rustic.

2 Cornish hens or guinea fowl, halved, backbone removed, wing tips trimmed

45g unsalted butter, melted

60ml olive oil

1 tablespoon sea salt

1 teaspoon paprika

1 small green cabbage, cut into 5cm chunks

4 medium potatoes, peeled and quartered

2 medium onions, sliced into wedges

Preheat the oven to 200°C. Pat the hens dry with paper towels.

In a small dish, whisk together the melted butter, oil, salt and paprika to make a marinade.

In a large bowl, combine the cabbage, potatoes and onions. Toss with half of the marinade until evenly coated.

Place the hens in a separate dish and pour over the remaining marinade. Rub the marinade into the flesh with your fingers.

Place the cabbage, potatoes, and onions in a 23 by 33cm roasting pan. Nestle the hens on top of the vegetables and roast, uncovered, for 35 to 40 minutes until the hens are cooked through and the potatoes are tender. Take out of the oven and put under the grill for 3 to 4 minutes to crisp up the chicken skin.

PECHENA
PILESHKO I

BAKED CHICKEN WITH VEGETABLES

ZELENCHUK

This is a great meal for the summer months. As a young working mother, I love one-dish meals. My children love their vegetables sliced into rounds like little coins.

1 red onion, sliced

3 carrots, peeled and finely sliced into rounds

3 courgettes, finely sliced into rounds

3 garlic cloves, finely sliced

4 bone-in, skin-on chicken breast halves

MARINADE

60ml olive oil

1 tablespoon coarsely chopped fresh oregano

¼ teaspoon dried chilli flakes

½ teaspoon paprika

Zest of 1 lemon

2 teaspoons sea salt

1 teaspoon freshly ground black pepper

Preheat the oven to 200°C.

In a small bowl, whisk together the marinade ingredients.

In a large bowl, combine the onion, carrots, courgette and garlic. Pour half of the marinade over the vegetables and toss to coat. Spread the vegetables evenly in a 23 by 33cm baking dish.

Place the chicken breasts in a large bowl and pour the remaining marinade over them. Toss to coat and place the chicken breasts (skin side up) on top of the vegetables in the baking dish.

Roast, uncovered, for 30 to 35 minutes until the chicken is cooked through and brown and the vegetables are tender.

Take out of the oven and put under the grill for 3 to 4 minutes, watching carefully, to crisp up the chicken skin.

PILESHKO SO PECHURKI
CHICKEN & MUSHROOMS

*Many varieties of mushrooms grow wild throughout the regions of Macedonia.
Cremini or button mushrooms are still among the most common cooking
mushrooms, but the Boletus family mushrooms, found predominantly in the
oak forests, are also widely used. It is the same variety as the porcini or penny
bun mushroom and, if you can find them fresh (not dried and reconstituted),
I highly recommend trying them in this recipe.*

2 tablespoons extra-virgin
    olive oil
2 leeks (white and light green
    parts only), sliced into
    6mm rings
2 garlic cloves,
    coarsely chopped
1½ teaspoons sea salt
½ teaspoon paprika
½ teaspoon cinnamon
½ teaspoon freshly ground
    black pepper
280g sliced Cremini or button
    mushrooms
240ml red wine
250g tinned tomatoes
4–6 medium potatoes,
    peeled and cut into
    5cm pieces
6 boneless skinless chicken
    thighs, halved

Preheat the oven to 190°C.

In a large Dutch oven, heat the oil over medium heat. Add the leeks and
sauté until tender, 3 to 4 minutes. Stir in the garlic, salt, paprika, cinnamon
and black pepper and sauté for an additional 2 minutes.

Add the mushrooms and cook, stirring constantly, for 5 minutes until they
begin to soften. Pour in the wine and simmer until it has reduced by half,
4 to 5 minutes.

Add the tomatoes. Bring to a simmer and fold in the potatoes so they are
coated. Gently nestle the chicken between the potatoes and mushrooms in
the pot.

Cover with a lid or foil and bake in the oven for 20 minutes. Remove the lid
and bake for an additional 20 to 25 minutes, until the chicken is fully cooked
and the potatoes are tender.

RIBA
Fish

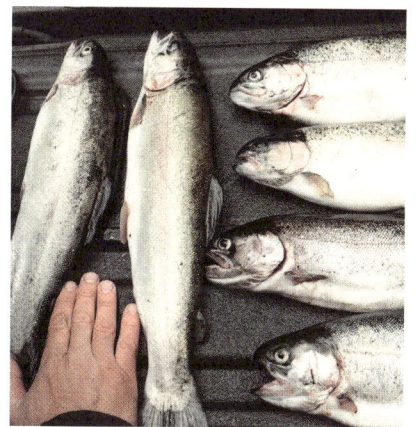

RIBA
Fish

Although much of Macedonia's regional cuisine is heavily influenced by the Mediterranean, the country is geographically landlocked, so seafood like shellfish and squid are not part of the traditional cuisine. Instead, our fish dishes come from Macedonia's bountiful lakes and rivers, which are a source of freshwater fish such as trout, rainbow trout and carp. Since these types of fish aren't always available outside North Macedonia, I recreated these recipes using fish with similar flavours and textures.

PECHENA SKUSHA
BAKED WHOLE MACKEREL

This is a very traditional way to cook fish in Macedonia. In 2002, I travelled to my parents' villages with them for the first time. We visited my aunt and uncle's holiday home, where, overlooking the beautiful mountains and amid the tranquility of the land, we feasted on beautiful baked whole fish that was freshly caught from the lake earlier that day.

4 medium-size whole mackerel, cleaned and trimmed

2 tablespoons extra-virgin olive oil, plus extra for greasing

1 medium onion, finely sliced

2 garlic cloves, minced

¼ teaspoon crushed chilli flakes

1 teaspoon freshly ground black pepper

240ml dry white wine

125ml warm water

1 medium tomato, peeled and diced

4 thin lemon slices

Sea salt

Preheat the oven to 180°C. Choose a baking dish large enough for the fish to lay flat, and grease it with olive oil.

Rinse and pat the fish dry. Arrange the fish flat in the baking dish. Brush the skins with 1 tablespoon of the olive oil and sprinkle with ½ teaspoon of salt. Set aside.

In a small sauté pan, heat 1 tablespoon of the olive oil over medium-high heat. Add the onion and sauté until tender, 3 to 4 minutes. Stir in the garlic, chilli flakes, 2 teaspoons of salt and the black pepper. Sauté for an additional 2 minutes.

Reduce the heat to medium. Pour in the wine and simmer until it has reduced by half, 4 to 5 minutes. Add the warm water and simmer for an additional 5 minutes.

Pour the onion and tomato mixture over the fish, leaving the head and tail slightly exposed. Place one lemon slice on top of each fish.

Cover the baking dish with a lid or foil and bake for 15 minutes. Remove the lid or foil and bake for an additional 12 to 15 minutes, until the fish is cooked through.

PRZHENI FILETI OD RIBA

FRIED FISH FILLETS

This is one of my favourite ways to eat fish. Pan-fried fish is commonplace throughout Macedonia, and you can really use any fish you like. I love a meaty fish but a delicate fish would work just as well in this recipe.

125g plain flour

2 teaspoons salt

1 teaspoon paprika

2 teaspoons coarsely chopped dill

4 firm white fish fillets, such as cod, halibut, bass or haddock, skin removed

60ml vegetable oil, for frying

4–6 lemon wedges, for garnish

In a shallow dish, mix together the flour, salt, paprika and 1 teaspoon of the chopped dill.

Coat each fish fillet in the seasoned flour and shake off any excess. Set aside.

In a large sauté pan, heat the oil until it begins to shimmer and reaches a temperature of about 180°C.

Carefully place the fish fillets in the oil and fry for 3 to 4 minutes on each side until golden brown.

Just before the fish is fully cooked, sprinkle the fillets with the remaining teaspoon of chopped dill. Transfer the fish to a plate lined with paper towels to drain excess oil.

Place the fillets on a serving dish and garnish with lemon wedges.

iVBORw0KGg

SERVES 4 TO 6

MARINARANA
RIBA NA
SKARA

GRILLED MARINATED FISH SKEWERS

These fish skewers are inspired by the street vendors of Macedonia's lakeside villages and towns. I love to make them with a selection of mezze dishes when friends are coming over in the afternoon. I keep them marinated and pre-skewered in the fridge and just grill a few at a time throughout the day as we relax and graze on various dishes. You will need 8 to 10 metal or pre-soaked bamboo skewers (soak bamboo skewers for 20 minutes).

FISH | 165 vertical

1 garlic clove
6g fresh mint
6g fresh parsley
1 teaspoon sea salt
½ teaspoon freshly ground
   black pepper
60ml extra-virgin olive oil
Juice of ½ lemon
900g firm white fish fillets
   such as halibut, bass or
   swordfish, cut into 2.5cm
   chunks
1 medium red onion, cut into
   2.5cm pieces

In a blender, purée the garlic, mint, parsley, salt, black pepper, olive oil and lemon juice to make a marinade.

Place the fish in a large bowl. Pour the marinade over the fish and gently toss to coat. Refrigerate for 1 hour to marinate.

Remove the fish from the refrigerator and alternately thread 3 pieces of fish and 2 pieces of onion onto each skewer.

Heat a grill pan or grill to medium-high heat. Grill the fish for 3 to 4 minutes on each side until golden brown cooked through.

Serve immediately.

RIBA SO LIMON

GRILLIED FISH WITH LEMON

This is a healthy, delicious way to enjoy any type of fish. I love to use large fillets of fish from my fishmonger. It is ridiculously easy to make and so impressive to serve. You can use any fish you like.

30g unsalted butter, melted

2 teaspoons olive oil, plus extra for greasing

1½ teaspoons sea salt

½ teaspoon freshly ground black pepper

1 teaspoon finely chopped fresh parsley

Zest of 1 lemon

Juice of ½ lemon

900g fillet of black cod or other flaky fish

Grilled or fresh lemon slices, for garnish (optional)

In a bowl, whisk together the melted butter, olive oil, salt, black pepper, parsley, lemon zest and lemon juice to make a marinade.

Grease a baking sheet with olive oil. Place the fish on the greased baking sheet (skin side down) and pour over the marinade. Cover the fish with cling film and refrigerate for 1 hour.

Preheat your grill to a medium heat.

Grill the fish for 7 to 10 minutes until it is cooked through.

Garnish with grilled or fresh lemon slices.

POLNETI RIBA

STUFFED FISH

I love the simple elegance of this whole fish with rice filling. The presentation of the dish is just so beautiful. My Australian husband fell in love with this recipe when I first made it for him.

4 medium-size whole white fish, such as trout or mackerel, cleaned and trimmed

1 tablespoon extra-virgin olive oil

FILLING

15g unsalted butter

90g long-grain white rice, rinsed and drained

1 tablespoon extra-virgin olive oil, plus extra for greasing

1 medium tomato, seeds removed, finely diced

2 tablespoons finely chopped parsley

1 tablespoon finely chopped dill

Zest of 1 lemon

1 garlic clove, minced

¼ teaspoon freshly ground black pepper

Lemon wedges, for serving

Sea salt

In a small saucepan, melt the butter over medium-high heat. Add the rice and stir for 1 minute until just toasted. Pour in 240ml water and ½ teaspoon of salt. Bring to a boil. Cover with a lid, reduce the heat, and simmer gently without stirring for 15 to 17 minutes, or until all the water is absorbed and the rice is tender. Turn off the heat and let stand, covered, for 5 minutes.

To make the filling, transfer the rice to a large bowl. Add the olive oil, tomato, parsley, dill, lemon zest, garlic, ½ teaspoon of salt and the black pepper. Stir with a fork to incorporate. Set aside.

Preheat the oven to 200°C. Grease a baking sheet with olive oil.

Wash and pat the fish dry. Fill the cavity of each fish with about 3 heaped spoonfuls of filling. You can use a toothpick to seal the cavities of the fish, if you like.

Brush the tops of the fish with the olive oil and sprinkle them with ½ teaspoon of salt. Place the fish on the greased baking sheet and bake for 20 to 25 minutes until the skin has crisped slightly and the fish is cooked through.

Remove the toothpicks, if using, and serve immediately with lemon wedges.

FISH | **169**

PECHENA RIBA SO KOMPIRI

BAKED FISH & POTATOES

My children and nephews love this dish because the mild-flavoured fish almost melts in your mouth. My grandmother used to make it for my sister and me when we were children, and now I love to make it for our children.

450g medium white potatoes, peeled

4 firm white fish fillets (such as sole, cod, halibut, bass or haddock), skin removed

¼ teaspoon freshly ground black pepper

1 tablespoon chopped fresh oregano

Zest of 1 lemon

1 medium tomato, cut into 6mm thick slices

1 tablespoon extra-virgin olive oil, plus extra for greasing

Sea salt

Place the potatoes in a medium stockpot and add a litre of cold water and 1 tablespoon of salt. Bring to a boil over high heat. Reduce the heat to medium and simmer for 10 minutes. Drain in a colander and toss well to shake off excess water. Set aside to cool.

Preheat the oven to 200°C. Grease a 23cm square baking dish with olive oil.

Cut the potatoes into slices 6mm thick. Arrange half of the potatoes in the bottom of the baking dish in one layer.

Arrange the fish fillets over the potatoes. Sprinkle the fish with ½ teaspoon of salt, the black pepper, half of the oregano and half of the lemon zest.

Layer the tomato slices over the fish and arrange the remaining potato slices on top. Sprinkle with the remaining oregano and lemon zest and drizzle with the olive oil.

Bake uncovered for 30 to 35 minutes until the potatoes are golden and tender and the fish is cooked.

ZELENCHUK

Vegetables & Side Dishes

ZELENCHUCK
Vegetables & Side Dishes

Family meals in Macedonia are typically robust and usually comprise a multitude of dishes. Rich in agriculture, the land provides an abundance of fruits and vegetables, which have inspired a wonderful selection of vibrant dishes. Most of the ingredients are native to Macedonia, but over centuries of trade, a few non-native ingredients have made a lasting impression. Rice has become an important part of the cuisine, a sign of the strong, enriching influence of the east.

TAVCHE
GRAVCHE

TRADITIONAL WHITE BEAN STEW

This is Macedonia's national dish, appearing on the table for weekday meals and celebrations alike. It is almost always served on Christmas Eve and for weddings and funerals. A simple dish of stewed beans and red peppers, it goes well with numerous meat, poultry and fish dishes, but is just as good on its own with crusty bread. It is not fancy or extravagant, but captures the true essence of traditional Macedonian cuisine.

370g dried cannellini beans,
soaked for at least
6 hours in plenty of water

15g unsalted butter

1 medium onion, diced

1 red pepper, diced

1 teaspoon paprika

2 tablespoons plain flour

1 litre boiling water

1 tablespoon sea salt

2 teaspoons chopped
fresh mint

2 teaspoons chopped
fresh parsley

Drain and rinse the beans and place them in a medium stockpot with 2 litres of fresh water.

Bring to a boil over high heat. Reduce the heat to medium and simmer, uncovered, for 30 minutes, until tender. Drain and set aside.

Preheat the oven to 190°C.

In a Dutch oven, melt the butter over medium heat. Add the onion, red pepper and paprika. Sauté until the vegetables are tender, 3 to 4 minutes.

Sprinkle in the flour and stir to coat the vegetables. Sauté for an additional 2 minutes.

Pour in the boiling water, salt and beans. Gently stir and bring to a simmer. Cover with a lid or foil and braise in the oven for 1 hour.

Sprinkle with mint and parsley and bake, uncovered, for another 30 minutes. Serve hot or at room temperature.

PECHENI KOMPIRI
ROASTED POTATOES

Everyone in my family makes their own version of roasted potatoes. Although they are all delicious, I developed my own favourite way. I love a really crispy exterior and soft and buttery interior, with a hint of fresh lemon. To create my perfect roasted potatoes, I first parboil the potatoes to soften the interiors and "fluff" the exteriors prior to roasting. They go with any main dish in this book.

4–6 starchy potatoes, such as
   Maris Piper, peeled
   and halved
3 tablespoons extra-virgin
   olive oil
1 teaspoon paprika
Juice of ½ lemon
Sea salt

Preheat the oven to 200°C.

Place the potatoes in a large stockpot with 2 litres of water and 1 tablespoon of salt. Bring to a boil over high heat, then reduce the heat to medium and simmer for 5 minutes.

Drain the potatoes and toss vigorously in a colander until they are dry and start to develop a fluffy exterior.

Transfer the potatoes to a heat resistant bowl. Toss them with the oil, paprika and 1 tablespoon of salt. Transfer the potatoes to a roasting pan large enough to accommodate them loosely in a single layer.

Roast in the oven for 40 to 45 minutes, until golden brown and tender when pierced with a knife.

Remove from the oven and sprinkle the lemon juice over the potatoes just before serving.

PILAV OD
ORIZ
RICE PILAF

Rice has an important role in Macedonian cuisine. Its mild character complements many of the salads and proteins. I'm a purist when it comes to rice. My grandfather taught me that first toasting the rice in a little butter and using boiling water instead of cold will keep the rice from sticking together, and it will cook perfectly every time.

280g long-grain white rice, rinsed and drained

45g unsalted butter

½ small onion, finely diced

700ml boiling water

1 teaspoon sea salt

In a medium saucepan, melt the butter over medium-high heat. Add the onion and sauté for 3 to 4 minutes until tender.

Add the rice to the pot and stir for 1 minute until just toasted.

Pour in the boiling water and salt, cover the pot and simmer for 15 to 17 minutes, until the water is fully absorbed and the rice is tender. Remove from the heat and let stand, covered, for 5 minutes.

Fluff with a fork and transfer to a serving dish.

PRZHENI
FRIED AUBERGINES
PATLIJANI

This is a popular dish in restaurants in Macedonia. The Macedonian style of eating usually has lots of small plates and side dishes around a centrepiece of meat or fish. Fried aubergines are an important part of that tapestry.

125g plain flour

115g plain dried breadcrumbs

3 eggs, beaten

1 medium tomato, seeds removed, finely diced

1 teaspoon coarsely chopped fresh mint

Zest of 1 lemon

2 medium aubergines, sliced in 6mm rounds

60ml vegetable oil

Sea salt and freshly ground black pepper

Pour the flour into a shallow dish with 1½ teaspoons of salt and 1 teaspoon of black pepper and stir to combine. In a second shallow dish, combine the breadcrumbs with 1½ teaspoons of salt and 1 teaspoon of black pepper. Place the beaten eggs in a third shallow dish.

In a small bowl, toss together the tomato, mint and lemon zest. Set aside.

Coat an aubergine slice in the flour, shaking off the excess. Then dip it into the eggs and shake off the excess. Finally, coat the aubergine slice with the breadcrumbs. Repeat with the rest of the aubergine slices and set aside.

In a large sauté pan, heat the oil until it begins to shimmer. Working in batches, carefully place the aubergine slices into the oil and fry until golden brown, about 4 minutes on each side. Transfer the fried aubergine slices to a plate lined with paper towels to drain excess oil.

Arrange the aubergine slices on a serving dish and garnish with the tomato, mint and lemon zest. Serve immediately.

BORANJA
BARIVO SO

STEWED GREEN BEANS WITH TOMATOES & ROASTED RED PEPPERS

ZARZAVAT

These are typically served alongside meat or fish dishes, but I love them on their own, too. I make this dish nearly every week, and I often double the recipe to have some in the fridge. They make a fantastic lunch, served cold with a chunk of feta cheese and a drizzle of olive oil. Sometimes I add a diced potato or some mushrooms if I have them on hand.

2 red peppers

2 medium tomatoes, peeled and coarsely chopped

1 teaspoon tomato purée

2 tablespoons extra-virgin olive oil

1 onion, finely diced

3 garlic cloves, minced

¼ teaspoon crushed chilli flakes

240ml red wine

900g green beans, washed and trimmed

2 teaspoons sea salt

1 teaspoon freshly ground black pepper

Roast the peppers over a BBQ or gas flame until the skins are completely charred and blistered. Alternatively put them under a hot grill (directly on the rack, or on a baking sheet lined with parchment paper), rotating them every 15 minutes until charred, for 30 to 45 minutes.

Place the peppers in a paper bag or heatproof container. Seal and let stand for 20 minutes until cool. Peel off the skins and remove the stems and seeds. Roughly chop the peppers and place them in a blender. Add the tomatoes and tomato purée and blitz for about 30 seconds. Set aside.

In a large stockpot, heat the oil over medium-high heat. Add the onion and sauté for 3 to 4 minutes until tender. Stir in the garlic and chilli flakes and sauté for an additional 2 minutes. Pour in the red wine and simmer until the wine has reduced by half, 4 to 5 minutes. Add the green beans to the pot. Pour the tomato and red pepper mixture over the beans and add the salt and pepper. Using tongs, toss the beans in the sauce until evenly coated.

Reduce the heat to low. Cover the pot with a lid and simmer for 50 to 60 minutes until the beans are soft and the sauce has thickened.

ZELKA SO KOPAR

CABBAGE WITH DILL

*This wilted cabbage is a perfect side dish with grilled meats,
especially Kremenadli (Grilled Pork Chops, page 110). I love what
happens to cabbage when it is cooked down in this way; it takes
on an almost noodle-like texture.*

15g unsalted butter

1 medium onion, sliced

1 garlic clove, minced

1½ teaspoons sea salt

1 green cabbage, cored and
thinly sliced

½ teaspoon red wine vinegar

2 teaspoons chopped fresh dill

In a large sauté pan, melt the butter over medium-high heat. Add the onion
and sauté for 3 to 4 minutes until tender. Stir in the garlic and salt and
sauté for an additional 2 minutes.

Reduce the heat to medium, add the cabbage and sauté until the cabbage
begins to wilt, about 10 minutes.

Remove from the heat. Stir in the red wine vinegar and dill and serve
immediately.

PRZHENI KOMPIRI
FRIED POTATOES

These were our potato chips growing up. My father would make these for us as a late-night snack when we were watching a movie or playing board games. I highly recommend crumbling feta cheese over the top, which is my favourite way to eat them.

½ teaspoon sea salt

½ teaspoon paprika

60ml vegetable oil, for frying

4–5 large starchy potatoes, such as russet or Maris Piper, peeled and sliced into 6mm rounds

Crumbled feta cheese, for serving (optional)

In a small dish, mix together the salt and paprika.

In a large sauté pan, heat the oil until it begins to shimmer.

Working in batches to avoid crowding the pan, carefully place the potato slices into the oil. Fry for 3 to 5 minutes on each side until golden brown and cooked through. Transfer the potatoes to a plate lined with paper towels to drain excess oil, then sprinkle them with the salt and paprika.

Place on a serving dish and sprinkle with crumbled feta cheese, if desired.

PECHENA TIKVA
ROASTED ACORN SQUASH

There are several different squash varieties that grow in Macedonia, but acorn squash is among the most common. Growing up in Toronto, we were fortunate to have access to incredible squash. Acorn squash is one of my favourites. In Macedonia, squash is often prepared simply, roasted like this, or boiled and puréed as a filling for savoury pastries. We only eat this in the fall when squash is in season and at its most flavourful.

2 acorn squash, quartered and deseeded

60g unsalted butter

½ teaspoon sea salt

¼ teaspoon cinnamon

¼ teaspoon nutmeg

Preheat the oven to 190°C.

Place the squash (cut side up) on a baking sheet.

In a small saucepan, melt the butter and add the salt, cinnamon and nutmeg.

Brush the squash with the melted butter and roast in the oven for 45 to 60 minutes, or until easily pierced with a fork.

KOMPIR KOLACHI

POTATO CAKES

We loved to have these with saucy stews like Govedsko Meso So Kromit (Beef and Onion Stew, page 121). My mother would place one potato cake in the bottom of the bowl and ladle the stew over the top. Made a little smaller, these can also be served as mezze.

5–6 Maris Piper potatoes, peeled and cut into chunks

2 eggs, beaten

60g plain flour

50g spring onions, thinly sliced

75g feta cheese, grated

1 teaspoon paprika

1 tablespoon finely chopped dill

60ml vegetable oil, for frying

Sea salt

Place the potatoes into a pot of cold water with 1 tablespoon of salt and bring to a boil. Reduce the heat to medium and boil until cooked through, 7 to 10 minutes.

Drain the potatoes and set aside until cool and dry. In a large bowl, mash the potatoes or pass through a potato ricer until smooth. Add the eggs, flour, spring onions, feta, paprika, dill and 2 teaspoons of sea salt and mix until fully incorporated.

Form the mixture into cakes about 1cm thick and 6cm in diameter (or any size you like).

In a large frying pan, heat the oil over medium-high heat until it begins to shimmer.

Working in batches, carefully place the potato cakes in the hot oil and fry for 3 to 4 minutes on each side, until golden brown.

Transfer the cooked potato cakes to a plate lined with paper towels to drain excess oil.

Serve hot.

PECHEN
ZELENCHUK

ROASTED VEGETABLES

This is a simple medley of vegetables that grew in our garden. It is my go-to recipe for potlucks and large gatherings because it can sit at room temperature for a few hours. I often make a double or triple batch, just to keep in the fridge. The flavourful veggies make an excellent lunch with a chunk of feta cheese or a fried egg on top.

1 medium aubergine, peeled in stripes and cut into 1cm chunks

3 medium courgettes, cut into 1cm rounds

3 peppers (red, yellow, or orange), cut into 2.5cm chunks

300g cherry tomatoes, halved

2 large red onions, peeled and cut into 1cm wedges

SAUCE

3 garlic cloves, peeled and coarsely chopped

1 tablespoon chopped fresh mint

1 tablespoon chopped fresh oregano

120ml olive oil

1 tablespoon sea salt

2 teaspoons freshly ground black pepper

Zest of 1 lemon

Preheat the oven to 190°C.

Make the sauce: In a blender, purée the garlic, mint, oregano, olive oil, salt, black pepper and lemon zest.

Place the prepared vegetables in a large roasting pan. Pour the sauce over the vegetables and toss to coat.

Roast for 40 to 50 minutes until the vegetables are tender.

KAIGANA
SO PIPERKI I
PEPPER & TOMATO SCRAMBLED EGGS
DOMATI

This is a proper Macedonian breakfast. This recipe is so satisfying and can be spicy or mild depending on the peppers you use.

½ tablespoon unsalted butter

3 banana peppers, deseeded and sliced into 6mm thick rings

4 small tomatoes, diced

¼ teaspoon sea salt

¼ teaspoon ground black pepper

8 eggs, beaten

40g feta cheese, grated

½ teaspoon coarsely chopped fresh parsley

Sliced crusty bread, toasted

In a large frying pan, melt the butter over medium-high heat. Add the peppers and sauté until tender, 3 to 4 minutes. Add the tomatoes and sauté for an additional 2 to 3 minutes. Stir in the salt and black pepper.

Pour in the eggs. Using a spatula, push the edge of the eggs towards the centre, working your way around the pan until the eggs are just cooked. Transfer to serving plates.

Sprinkle with the feta cheese and parsley and serve with warm toast.

LEB
Breads

LEB

Breads

Bread and baked goods are a most celebrated and important component of Macedonian cuisine. For my father, like for many Macedonians, bread is the fourth utensil, soaking up all the rich flavours of every meal. It is not just a staple of daily life; it also plays an important part of almost all celebrations, playing a symbolic role in wedding ceremonies, birth celebrations, baptisms, funerals, and Christmas, New Year's and Easter traditions.

POGACHA
BRAIDED RICH BREAD

This is the bread of all breads in Macedonian cuisine. It plays a role in almost all of our most important traditions, including baptisms, weddings and funerals. Traditionally, the bride and groom tear apart the Pogacha as part of their wedding ceremony—whoever gets the bigger piece is said to rule the household. But it is also an ideal day-to-day bread, and often portioned into simple loaves. My grandmother could make this bread using just her instincts to measure the ingredients.

120ml warm water

7g fast action dried yeast

50g plus ½ teaspoon sugar

3 eggs

60ml vegetable oil, plus extra for greasing

500g plain flour, sifted, plus extra for dusting

2 teaspoons sea salt

Sesame seeds, for garnish

Place the warm water in a bowl and add the yeast and ½ teaspoon sugar. Stir once. Cover the bowl with a plate and let stand until the yeast begins to foam, about 10 minutes.

In another small bowl, whisk together 2 of the eggs and the oil.

In a large bowl, whisk together the flour, salt and 50g of sugar. Make a well in the centre.

Pour the yeast and egg mixtures into the centre of the well. Using a spatula, gently fold the flour into the liquid until incorporated and a dough begins to form. Transfer the dough to a lightly floured work surface and knead for about 10 minutes until it is smooth and elastic. Dust the surface of the dough with extra flour if it feels sticky.

Lightly grease a large bowl with vegetable oil and place the dough inside. Brush the top of the dough with a thin layer of vegetable oil. Cover the bowl with a large plate or tea towel and set aside in a warm place to rise for 1 hour, or until doubled in size. Grease a 23cm round baking tin with vegetable oil and set aside.

Return the dough to your lightly floured work surface and divide it into 3 equal portions. Roll the dough into 3 ropes, each about 40cm long and 5cm thick. Attach the 3 ropes together at the top end and carefully braid them.

Coil the braided dough into a circle and place it in the greased tin. Tuck the ends of the braid under the coil. Brush the top of the dough with oil, cover loosely with a tea towel, and set in a warm place to rise for an additional 30 minutes.

Preheat the oven to 180°C.

Whisk the remaining egg and use it to brush the top of the dough, then sprinkle with sesame seeds.

Bake for 30 minutes, then reduce the heat to 135°C and bake for an additional 15 to 20 minutes, or until golden. Let the bread cool before removing it from the tin.

When my husband and I got married, we had a small celebration in Toronto for family who wouldn't be able to travel to Los Angeles for our larger wedding the following year. My grandmother made us Pogacha, and I tore the largest piece. In LA, we found a local baker to make us a large decorated loaf. They took the "large" part literally and you could barely lift it! In this challenge, my husband won the bigger piece, but we joke that my grandmother's Pogacha is the only one that really mattered.

PCHENKARNI LEB

CORNBREAD

My grandfather always said this bread reminded him of the village. Corn grew well in my father's village and the stalks were used to feed the animals. The kernels were ground for bread, which was made weekly in wood-fired ovens (furna). It is similar in texture to American-style cornbread, but a bit less sweet.

160g plain flour
120g medium-ground yellow
  cornmeal
50g sugar
1 tablespoon baking powder
½ teaspoon sea salt
1 egg
240ml whole milk
1 tablespoon honey
60g unsalted butter, melted,
  plus extra for greasing

Preheat the oven to 190°C. Grease a 20cm square cake tin with butter and set aside.

Sift the flour into a large bowl, and add the cornmeal, sugar, baking powder and salt, and whisk to incorporate.

In another bowl, whisk together the egg, milk and honey. Slowly mix in the melted butter.

Pour the wet ingredients into dry ingredients and gently whisk just until the flour is incorporated. Be careful not to over-mix.

Pour the batter into the prepared tin and bake for 30 minutes until golden brown.

Remove from the oven and let cool slightly before serving.

KOZINAK
EASTER BREAD

In the week leading up to Easter, my mother, sister and I always made about 30 loaves of Kozinak. As per tradition, we wrapped each small loaf up with a few eggs (usually dyed red and yellow) and some chocolates, and gave one parcel to each of our neighbours, friends and family members. In turn, we received multiple loaves from other families. Luckily, this bread freezes well and can be enjoyed for weeks after Easter. Its key ingredient is mahleb, a spice that comes from the ground pit of a species of cherry tree called St. Lucie. If you can't find it, you can substitute vanilla extract.

120ml warm water

7g fast action dried yeast

200g plus ½ teaspoon sugar

625g plain flour, sifted, plus extra for dusting

½ teaspoon sea salt

113g unsalted butter, melted

120ml warm whole milk

4 eggs

Juice and zest of 1 medium orange

1 teaspoon ground *mahleb*, or 1 tablespoon vanilla extract

Vegetable oil, for greasing

Sesame seeds, for garnish

Place the warm water in a small bowl and add the yeast and ½ teaspoon sugar, and stir once. Cover the bowl with a plate and let stand until the yeast begins to foam, about 10 minutes.

In a large bowl, whisk together the flour and salt and make a well in the centre.

In another bowl, whisk together the melted butter, milk, 200g sugar, 3 of the eggs, orange juice, orange zest and *mahleb*.

Pour the melted butter and milk mixture into the centre of the well. Using a spatula, gently fold the flour into the liquid until incorporated and a dough begins to form. Transfer the dough to a lightly floured work surface and knead for about 10 minutes until it is smooth and elastic. Dust the surface of the dough with extra flour if it starts to feel sticky.

Lightly grease a large bowl with vegetable oil and place the dough inside. Brush the top of the dough with a thin layer of vegetable oil. Cover the bowl with a large plate or tea towel and set aside in a warm place to rise for 2 hours, or until doubled in size.

Grease 2 loaf tins with vegetable oil.

Return the dough to your lightly floured work surface and divide it into 6 equal portions. Roll each portion into a rope about 25cm long. Attach 3 of the ropes together at the top end and carefully braid them. Tuck the ends of the braid under the loaf and place it into a greased loaf tin. Repeat with the remaining 3 ropes so you have two loaves. Brush the tops of the loaves with oil, cover loosely with cling film, and set aside in a warm place to rise again for 30 minutes.

Preheat the oven to 180°C.

Whisk the remaining egg, and use it to brush the top of each loaf. Sprinkle the loaves with sesame seeds.

Bake for 25 to 30 minutes until golden brown and cooked through. Remove from oven and let cool for 10 minutes before removing from the tin.

POLNETI
STUFFED CRESCENT ROLLS
KIFLICHKI

My parents still live in the house where they brought me home from the hospital. Another Macedonian family lived next door, and we all grew up together. Every few months, a few of the Macedonian families in our neighbourhood would get together for a meal, and my "aunt" Mitra next door made these better than anyone I know. I was fortunate to have her help with this recipe.

240ml warm water

7g fast action dried yeast

½ teaspoon sugar

625g plain flour, sifted, plus extra for dusting

1 tablespoon sea salt

240ml warm whole milk

120ml vegetable oil, plus extra for greasing

3 eggs

FILLING

2 eggs

225g feta cheese, grated

120g ricotta cheese

¼ teaspoon sea salt

Grease 2 large baking sheets with vegetable oil.

Place the warm water in a small bowl and add the yeast and sugar. Cover with a plate and let stand until the yeast begins to foam, about 10 minutes.

In a large bowl, whisk together the flour and salt and make a well in the centre. In a separate bowl, whisk together the milk, oil and 2 of the eggs.

Pour the yeast and egg mixtures into the centre of the well. Using a spatula, gently fold the flour into the liquid until incorporated and a dough begins to form. Transfer the dough to a lightly floured work surface and knead for about 10 minutes until it is smooth and elastic. Dust the surface of the dough with extra flour if it feels sticky.

Divide the dough into 4 equal portions. Form each portion into a ball and place them on one of the greased baking sheets. Brush the tops of the balls of dough with vegetable oil. Loosely cover with a tea towel and set aside in a warm place to rise for 10 minutes.

Meanwhile, mix together the filling ingredients and set aside.

Roll out each ball into a circle 40cm in diameter and about 6mm thick. Using a knife or a pizza cutter, cut the dough into 8 triangles.

Place one triangle in front of you, with the wide edge closest to you. Place about 1 tablespoon of the filling on the wide edge. Fold the dough over the filling once and pinch the edges closed. Roll the dough up until the point of the triangle is wrapped over the roll. Gently pull the tips of the roll towards each other to form a crescent shape and place on a prepared baking sheet. Repeat with the remaining dough and filling, spacing the crescents about 5cm apart on the sheets.

Brush the tops of the crescents with vegetable oil. Loosely cover the baking sheets with tea towels and set aside in a warm place to rise for 30 minutes.

Preheat the oven to 180°C. Whisk the remaining egg and use it to brush the tops of the crescents.

Bake for 25 to 30 minutes until golden brown (you may need to do this in batches if both baking sheets don't fit in your oven at once).

Best served warm. You can store them in an airtight container in the refrigerator for up to 2 days, or the freezer for up to 2 months. Reheat before serving.

PITA NA SKARA

GRILLED FLATBREAD

Along with Pogacha (Braided Rich Bread, page 202), pita is our most common daily bread, and almost always served alongside mezze, especially with dips. I make these grilled flatbreads a few times a week since my children love them. Freshly made, they go well with nearly everything.

7g fast action dried yeast

½ teaspoon sugar

350ml warm water

500g plain flour, sifted, plus extra for dusting

2 teaspoons sea salt

3 tablespoons extra-virgin olive oil, plus extra for greasing

Place the warm water in a small bowl and add the yeast and sugar. Cover the bowl with a plate and let stand until the yeast begins to foam, about 10 minutes.

In a large bowl, whisk together the flour and salt and make a well in the centre. Pour the yeast mixture and 3 tablespoons of olive oil into the centre of the well. Using a spatula, gently fold the flour into the liquid until incorporated and a dough begins to form. Transfer the dough to a lightly floured work surface and knead for about 10 minutes until it is smooth and elastic. Dust the surface with extra flour if the dough starts to feel sticky.

Lightly grease a large bowl with vegetable oil and place the dough inside. Brush the top of the dough with a thin layer of vegetable oil. Cover the bowl with a large plate or tea towel and set aside in a warm place to rise for 1 hour, or until doubled in size.

Return the dough to your work surface and divide into 16 equal portions. Using your hands, work them into rounds about 1cm thick and 20cm in diameter. Use a rolling pin if you want the breads to be thinner.

Heat a grill pan over medium-high heat and brush with olive oil. Place a dough round on the pan and cook for 2 to 3 minutes on each side until the grill marks are golden brown. Repeat with the remaining dough, brushing the grill pan with olive oil between each batch.

These are best served fresh, but you can freeze them for up to 2 months and reheat as needed.

LEB SO OREVI
WALNUT BREAD

This bread is hearty and comforting. One of my favourite breakfasts is a few toasted slices of walnut bread with butter and jam and a steaming cup of planenski chai *(mountain tea), made from a flower similar to chamomile that grows wild in the mountains of Macedonia.*

350ml warm water

6g fast action dried yeast

½ teaspoon sugar

60ml honey

2 tablespoons extra-virgin olive
  oil, plus extra for greasing

500g plain flour, sifted, plus
  extra for dusting

2 teaspoons sea salt

240g coarsely chopped
  walnuts

8 walnut halves, for garnish

Place the warm water in a small bowl and stir in the yeast and sugar. Cover the bowl with a plate and let stand until the yeast begins to foam, 10 minutes.

In another small bowl, whisk together the honey and oil.

In a large bowl, mix together the flour, salt and chopped walnuts. Make a well in the centre. Pour the yeast mixture and the honey mixture into the centre of the well. Using a spatula, gently fold the flour into the liquid until incorporated and a dough begins to form. Transfer the dough to a lightly floured work surface and knead for about 10 minutes until it is smooth and elastic. Dust the surface with extra flour if the dough starts to feel sticky.

Lightly grease a large bowl with vegetable oil and place the dough inside. Brush the top of the dough with a thin layer of vegetable oil. Cover the bowl with a large plate or tea towel and set aside in a warm place to rise for 1 hour, or until doubled in size.

Preheat the oven to 200°C. Grease a baking sheet with olive oil.

Return the dough to your work surface and gently shape it into a log about 45cm long, being careful not to overwork the dough. Mold the dough into a ring about 23cm in diameter, leaving a hole in the centre, and place the ring on the baking sheet. Press evenly spaced walnut halves into the top of the dough.

Bake for 10 minutes, then reduce the heat to 180°C and bake for an additional 40 minutes, until golden brown. It should have a crisp, hearty crust and a rich, dense interior.

POUPCHINA
BREAD ROLLS

Soft and airy, these little buns make great dinner rolls or sandwich bread.

120ml warm water

7g fast action dried yeast

3 tablespoons plus
½ teaspoon sugar

120ml whole milk

60g unsalted butter

2 eggs, beaten

500g plain flour, sifted, plus
extra for dusting

1 teaspoon sea salt

Vegetable oil for greasing

Place the warm water in a small bowl, add the yeast and ½ teaspoon of the sugar, and stir once. Cover the bowl with a plate and let stand until the yeast begins to foam, about 10 minutes.

In a small saucepan, bring the milk and butter to a simmer. Remove from the heat and set aside to cool until warm.

Place the eggs in a small bowl and, whisking constantly, slowly pour the milk and butter mixture into the eggs.

In a large bowl, combine the flour, salt and the 3 tablespoons of sugar. Make a well in the centre. Pour the yeast mixture and egg mixture into the centre of the well. Using a spatula, gently fold the flour into the liquid until incorporated and a dough begins to form. Transfer the dough to a lightly floured work surface and knead for about 10 minutes until smooth and elastic. Dust the surface with extra flour if the dough starts to feel sticky.

Lightly grease a large bowl with vegetable oil and place the dough inside. Brush the top of the dough with a thin layer of vegetable oil. Cover the bowl with a large plate or tea towel and set aside in a warm place to rise for 1 hour, or until doubled in size.

Grease a baking sheet with oil. Divide the dough into 8 equal portions. Form each portion into a smooth ball and place on the greased baking sheet. Brush each ball with oil. Loosely cover the baking sheet with a tea towel and set aside in a warm place to rise for an additional 30 minutes.

Preheat the oven to 180°C. Dust the tops of the dough with a little flour and bake for 20 minutes until golden brown. The rolls should be soft and fluffy.

GEVRETSI SO SUSAM

SESAME RINGS

These are much coveted, especially in the Kavadarci region of Macedonia. When we were children attending Macedonian language school, there was a lovely old man who sold them outside of the school, and we always stopped to have one. They are common in Macedonian bakeries and are popular as an afternoon snack.

180ml warm water

3g fast action dried yeast

2 tablespoons plus
½ teaspoon sugar

375g plain flour, sifted,
plus extra for dusting

2 teaspoons sea salt

2 tablespoons extra-virgin olive
oil, plus extra for greasing

2 egg whites, beaten

145g sesame seeds

Place the warm water in a small bowl, add the yeast and ½ teaspoon sugar and stir once. Cover the bowl with a plate and let stand until the yeast begins to foam, about 10 minutes.

In a large bowl, combine the flour, salt and the 2 tablespoons of sugar. Make a well in the centre.

Pour the yeast mixture and 2 tablespoons of olive oil into the centre of the well. Using a spatula, gently fold the flour into the liquid until incorporated and a dough begins to form. Transfer the dough to a lightly floured work surface and knead for about 10 minutes until it is smooth and elastic. Dust the surface with extra flour if the dough starts to feel sticky.

Lightly grease a large bowl with vegetable oil and place the dough inside. Brush the top of the dough with a thin layer of olive oil. Cover the bowl with a large plate or tea towel and set aside in a warm place to rise for 1 hour, until doubled in size.

Preheat the oven to 190°C. Grease 2 baking sheets with olive oil.

Transfer the dough to a clean work surface and divide it into 16 equal portions. Roll each portion into a log about 1cm thick and 20cm long.

Connect the ends of each log to form a ring. Place the rings on the greased baking sheets, spacing them 5cm apart and cover loosely with a tea towel. Set aside in a warm place to rise again for 30 minutes.

Brush each ring with the whisked egg whites and cover generously with sesame seeds.

Bake for 25 to 30 minutes until golden brown. (You may need to bake in batches if both baking sheets do not fit in your oven at once.)

BOUREK
FILLED PASTRY

Bourek is an institution in Macedonia. This filled pastry is found throughout the different regions and is known by different names. Depending on whether it is the tray-baked or coiled style, it is sometimes known as pita, kora, zelnik, or maznik. I have included the classic cheese filling, but fillings vary as well— you can find a variety of filling options (Bourek Plombi) on page 224. The standard for a great bourek is a flaky, buttery crust and delicious filling.

240ml warm water

3g fast action dried yeast

½ teaspoon sugar

375g plain flour, sifted, plus extra for dusting

¾ teaspoon sea salt

113g unsalted butter, melted

Vegetable oil, for greasing

FILLING

150g feta cheese, grated

240g ricotta cheese

¼ teaspoon sea salt

2 eggs

Grease a 23 by 33cm baking dish with melted butter. Also grease a large baking sheet with vegetable oil.

Mix together the filling ingredients and set aside in the refrigerator.

Place the warm water in a small bowl, add the yeast and sugar, and stir once. Cover the bowl with a plate and let stand until the yeast begins to foam, about 10 minutes.

In a large bowl, combine the flour and salt and make a well in the centre. Pour the yeast mixture into the centre of the well. Using a spatula, gently fold the flour into the liquid until incorporated and a dough begins to form.

Transfer the dough to a lightly floured work surface and knead for about 10 minutes until it is smooth and elastic. Dust the surface with extra flour if the dough starts to feel sticky.

Divide the dough into 8 equal portions and form each into a ball. Arrange the balls on the greased baking sheet, spaced about 8cm apart, and lightly brush each ball of dough with oil. Loosely cover the tray with a tea towel and leave in a warm place to rise for 1 hour, until about doubled in size.

Preheat the oven to 180°C.

On your work surface, roll out 4 of the balls into 13 by 18cm rectangles, each about 6mm thick. Brush 3 of the rectangles with melted butter and place one on top of the other. Place the fourth rectangle on top. Do not brush the top of the stack with butter.

On a lightly floured surface, use a rolling pin to roll the stack out to 6mm thick, and about 5cm larger than the bottom of your baking dish. Place the dough into the baking dish, with the edges hanging over the sides. Brush the top of the dough with melted butter. Spread the filling evenly on top, then fold in the edges of the dough over the filling.

Roll and stretch out one of the remaining balls of dough as thinly as you can, so it is just larger than the size of the baking dish. The dough should be almost transparent. Place this loosely over the top of the filling in the baking dish. Gently brush the top of the dough with butter. Repeat with the remaining 3 balls of dough, brushing the top of each layer with butter (including the top layer).

Bake for 40 to 50 minutes until golden brown and heated through. Allow to cool for 10 minutes before slicing it into squares.

BANITSA SO SIRENJE

FILLED COILED PASTRY

This is a traditionally Macedonian style of savoury pastry. The filled pastry is shaped into a coil and sliced like a pie. The cheese filling is most common, but you can find many other fillings on page 224.

240ml warm water

3g fast action dried yeast

½ teaspoon sugar

375g plain flour, sifted, plus extra for dusting

¾ teaspoon sea salt

113g unsalted butter, melted

Vegetable oil for greasing

FILLING

150g feta cheese, grated

240g ricotta cheese

¼ teaspoon sea salt

2 eggs

Grease 2 large baking sheets with vegetable oil.

Mix together the filling ingredients and set aside in the refrigerator.

Place the warm water in a small bowl, add the yeast and ½ teaspoon sugar, and stir once. Cover the bowl with a plate and let stand until the yeast begins to foam, about 10 minutes.

In a large bowl, combine the flour and salt and make a well in the centre. Pour the yeast mixture into the centre of the well. Using a spatula, gently fold the flour into the liquid until incorporated and a dough begins to form.

Transfer the dough to a lightly floured work surface and knead for about 10 minutes until it is smooth and elastic. Dust the surface with extra flour if the dough starts to feel sticky.

Divide the dough into 6 equal portions and form each into a ball. Arrange the balls on a greased baking sheet, about 8cm apart, and brush each ball of dough with a few drops of oil. Loosely cover with a tea towel and leave in a warm place to rise for 1 hour, until about doubled in size.

On your work surface, roll out 3 of the balls into 23 by 40cm rectangles, each about 6mm thick. Brush 2 of the rectangles with melted butter and place one on top of the other. Place the third rectangle on top. Do not brush the top of the stack with butter. Set aside.

Repeat with the remaining 3 pieces of dough, so you have 2 stacks, each made up of 3 layers. Cover loosely with a tea towel and let the dough rest for 20 minutes.

Preheat the oven to 180°C.

On your work surface, use a rolling pin to carefully and patiently roll out each stack of dough as thinly as possible into a rectangle about 45 by 80cm. You can also use your fingers to help stretch out the dough. It should be almost transparent. Don't worry if it tears slightly—when you assemble the coil, the holes will not be noticeable. Place the dough horizontally with the long side closest to you.

Place half of the filling along the long side of the dough closest to you, about 2.5cm from the edge. Fold the edge of the dough over the filling and roll it away from you into a rope. Curl the end and begin to wrap the rope around to form a coil. Carefully place the coil onto the first baking sheet. Repeat this process with the second piece of dough and place it on the second baking sheet.

Brush the top of each coil with melted butter and bake in the oven for 45 to 50 minutes, or until golden brown. (You may need to bake in batches if your oven can't fit both baking sheets at once.)

Allow to cool for 10 minutes before slicing into wedges.

LESNA BANITSA SO SIRENJE

EASY FILLED COILED PASTRY

I developed this recipe because, as much as I love the process of making Bourek *(page 218) or* Banitsa *(page 220), it is a labour of love and I don't always have the time. I experimented with rolling out store-bought puff pastry dough very thinly with flour, and the result is as close as you can get to the homemade dough. Find alternative fillings on page 224.*

450g package puff pastry
   sheets, thawed
Plain flour, for dusting
1 egg, beaten
Vegetable oil, for greasing

FILLING

150g feta cheese, grated
240g ricotta cheese
¼ teaspoon sea salt
2 eggs

Preheat the oven to 180°C. Grease a 23cm pie tin or oven-safe dish with vegetable oil.

Mix together the filling ingredients and set aside in the refrigerator.

Lightly dust your work surface with flour and use a rolling pin to roll out each sheet of puff pastry until it is 6mm thick, creating two long rectangles, each about 75cm long and about 30cm wide. Slice each sheet of pastry in half lengthwise. You will have 4 long strips of dough. Prick the surface of each strip at random with a fork.

Brush the dough strips with beaten egg. Spoon a quarter of the filling along the long side of one strip of dough, about 2.5cm from the edge of the dough. Fold the edge of the dough over the filling and roll it up to create a rope. Repeat with the remaining strips of dough.

Using a bit of beaten egg, gently pinch the ends of the ropes together to form one long rope. Form the rope into a coil and carefully place it in the pie tin. Brush the top with the remaining egg and bake for 45 to 50 minutes, until golden brown. Allow to cool for 10 minutes before slicing into wedges.

BOUREK PLOMBI
SAVOURY PASTRY FILLINGS

Using in-season ingredients is an important part of how Macedonians cook. Savoury pastries are made year-round with sirenje *(cheese) or* meso *(meat) fillings, but we typically use* pras *(leek) and* tikva *(pumpkin) in the fall, and* spanak *(spinach) and* kisela zelka *(sauerkraut) in the winter. These fillings can all be used for any of the savoury pastry dishes on pages 218–223. Each filling recipe is enough for one Bourek (Filled Pastry, page 218), Banitsa (Filled Coiled Pastry, page 220), or Lesna Banitsa (Easy Filled Coiled Pastry, page 223). I recommend trying them all.*

Spanak SPINACH

15g unsalted butter
100g coarsely chopped baby spinach
170g feta cheese, grated
120g ricotta cheese
1 egg
¼ teaspoon sea salt

In a large sauté pan, melt the butter and add the spinach. Toss to coat, just until the spinach begins to wilt and has turned bright green. Then immediately remove from the heat, and mix with the remaining ingredients. Refrigerate until needed.

Kisela Zelka SAUERKRAUT

15g unsalted butter
225g cans of sauerkraut, rinsed
   and drained
¼ teaspoon paprika
115g feta cheese, grated
1 egg

In a medium frying pan, melt the butter and sauté the sauerkraut with the paprika for 3 minutes until the liquid has evaporated. Remove from the heat and mix in the cheese and egg until fully incorporated. Refrigerate until needed.

Tikva PUMPKIN OR SQUASH

1–1.5kg pumpkin
  or squash, cut into 8 slices,
  seeds removed
120g ricotta cheese
1 egg
½ teaspoon sea salt
⅛ teaspoon nutmeg

Preheat the oven to 200°C.

Place the pumpkin slices on a baking sheet and bake in the oven for 30 to 40 minutes, until fork-tender. Remove and let cool. Peel off the skins and place the pumpkin flesh in a food processor. Purée until smooth.

Mix in the remaining ingredients until fully incorporated. Refrigerate until needed.

Pras LEEK

15g unsalted butter
2 leeks (white and light green
  parts only), finely sliced
170g feta cheese, grated
120g ricotta cheese
1 egg
¼ teaspoon sea salt
⅛ teaspoon finely ground
  black pepper

In a medium sauté pan, melt the butter and sauté the leeks for 3 to 4 minutes until translucent.

Remove from the heat and mix in the remaining ingredients until fully incorporated. Refrigerate until needed.

Meleno Meso MINCED MEAT

1 teaspoon extra-virgin olive oil
225g lean minced beef
225g lean minced pork
1 small onion, finely diced
½ red or green pepper,
  finely diced
1 teaspoon sea salt
½ teaspoon paprika
125g tinned tomatoes

Heat the oil in a large pan and brown the minced beef and pork, stirring constantly for about 4 minutes. Transfer the meat to a plate and drain the excess oil from the pan.

In the same pan, sauté the onion and pepper over high heat until tender, about 5 minutes. Stir in the salt and paprika and toss to coat. Add the tomatoes and return the meat to the pan. Reduce the heat to medium and simmer for 5 minutes. Allow to cool before using, or refrigerate until needed.

SLATKO

Sweets

SLATKO

Sweets

Many of Macedonia's classic desserts are heavily influenced
by the legacy of the Ottoman Empire. Honey, nuts, orange and
cinnamon are common flavourings. Macedonian sweets are
not very complicated to make, and generally go very well with
slivovitz (*plum brandy*), or planenski chai (*mountain tea*), a robust
chamomile-like tea sourced from the mountains of Macedonia.

BAKLAVA

FILO & WALNUT PASTRY

Baklava can be found throughout the Balkan Peninsula, as well as in Greece, Turkey, Armenia and the Middle East. The ingredients vary regionally, depending on what is available. Some use pistachios, pine nuts or hazelnuts, flavoured with cloves or rosewater. In Macedonia, baklava is traditionally made with walnuts and almonds, flavoured with cinnamon, orange and honey.

450g filo pastry

FILLING

200g walnut halves
140g almonds
50g sugar
2 teaspoons cinnamon
113g unsalted butter, melted

SYRUP

400g sugar
480ml water
60ml honey
1 cinnamon stick
1 tablespoon fresh orange juice

Preheat the oven to 180°C. Brush a 28 by 38cm baking tin with melted butter.

First, make the filling: In a food processor, combine the walnuts, almonds, sugar and cinnamon and pulse for 15 to 20 seconds until the filling is coarsely chopped. Set aside.

Remove the filo from its package and immediately cover it with a damp tea towel. Make sure to keep the filo covered to prevent it from drying out.

Place 1 sheet of filo on a clean work surface with the long side in front of you. Brush the surface very lightly with melted butter and place another sheet on top. Repeat so you have a stack of 3 buttered sheets. Spoon a strip of filling along the long side of the filo stack, about 2.5cm away from the edge. Fold the filo over the filling and roll into a long rope. Repeat this process with the remaining filo sheets and filling. Arrange the rolled ropes side by side in the buttered baking pan. Brush the tops of the rolls with butter.

Cut the uncooked rolls into serving-size pieces about 5cm long, straight across or diagonally. It is important to cut the baklava before baking. Bake the baklava for 30 to 45 minutes or until golden brown. Remove from the oven and let cool for about 20 minutes.

In a saucepan, combine the syrup ingredients and bring to a boil. Reduce the heat to low and simmer for 15 minutes, until thickened. Let the syrup cool for 5 minutes before pouring it over the cooled baklava.

TORTA SO KISELO MLEKO

SOUR CREAM CAKE

This is my mother's signature cake. She made this often and the aroma that would permeate our home was heavenly.

340g unsalted butter at room temperature, plus extra for greasing

300g sugar

3 eggs

350ml sour cream

280g plain flour, sifted

1½ teaspoons bicarbonate of soda

1 teaspoon baking powder

½ teaspoon sea salt

1 tablespoon icing sugar, for dusting

FILLING

100g light brown sugar

2 teaspoons cinnamon

100g finely chopped walnuts

Preheat the oven to 180°C. Grease a bundt or angel food cake tin with butter.

Using a stand mixer with the paddle attachment, or in a large bowl with a hand mixer on medium speed, combine the butter and sugar until fluffy, about 4 minutes. Whisk in the eggs and sour cream.

In a separate bowl, combine the flour, bicarbonate of soda, baking powder and salt.

Slowly mix the dry ingredients into the wet ingredients, mixing at medium speed until fully incorporated, about 2 minutes. You should have a thick batter.

In a separate bowl, combine all the filling ingredients.

Pour half of the cake batter into the pan and smooth the top with a spatula. Sprinkle the walnut filling on top in an even layer. Spoon the remaining batter on top of the filling, carefully smoothing the top with a spatula.

Bake for 45 minutes, until a skewer inserted into the centre comes out clean.

Allow to cool in the pan for 10 minutes. Turn out onto a serving plate, and let cool for an additional 10 minutes, before dusting with icing sugar.

SHTRUDLA SO KRUSHI
PEAR STRUDEL

This strudel can be made with any stewed fruit, like apples, cherries or plums, but my mother has always made it with pears. The sour cream might seem unusual, but I find it makes the pastry light and flaky.

DOUGH

375g plain flour, sifted, plus
  extra for dusting
225g cold unsalted butter,
  grated
120ml sour cream
1 egg yolk
1 whole egg, beaten,
  for egg wash

FILLING

60g unsalted butter
1 tablespoon flour
60ml brandy
70g light brown sugar
40g chopped dried apricots
30g chopped walnuts
1 teaspoon cinnamon
½ teaspoon sea salt
3-4 medium ripe pears, peeled
  cored and diced
1 tablespoon freshly squeezed
  lemon juice

In a large bowl, use your fingers to mix the flour and butter until it looks like coarse breadcrumbs. Use a spatula to fold in the sour cream and egg yolk. Lightly dust your work surface with flour and knead the mixture just until it comes together smoothly. Be careful not to overwork the dough. Flatten the dough into a rectangle about 13 by 25cm. Tightly wrap the dough in cling film and refrigerate for at least 2 hours or overnight.

When the dough has been chilled, preheat the oven to 180°C. Line a large baking sheet with parchment paper.

Make the filling: In a large sauté pan, melt the butter over medium heat. Slowly mix in the flour and stir until you have a roux. Add the brandy, sugar, apricots, walnuts, cinnamon and salt, and stir until the sugar dissolves. Fold in the pears, and simmer over medium heat for 5 minutes. Remove from the heat and add the lemon juice. Set aside to cool.

On a lightly floured surface, roll the dough into a rectangle 30 by 40cm and 6mm thick. Brush the top of the dough with some of the egg wash. Place the filling in a thick line down the centre of the rectangle. Fold each side of the dough over the filling, making sure the dough overlaps to create a seal. Carefully flip the strudel over and place it on the baking sheet, seam side down. Cut slits into the top of the dough about 2.5cm apart and brush the dough with the remaining egg wash.

Bake for 25 to 30 minutes, until golden brown.

KADAIF

SHREDDED FILO & ALMOND PASTRY

The origins of this dessert lie in the Middle East, but it is much loved in Macedonia. It is crunchy, nutty, sweet and so much simpler than it looks! I felt intimidated making Kadaif for the first time, but it really comes together quite easily.

480g shredded filo dough
(*kadaif*), thawed
113g unsalted butter, melted
Vegetable oil, for greasing

FILLING

45g finely chopped almonds
70g light brown sugar
30g dried breadcrumbs
1 egg, beaten
½ teaspoon cinnamon
Pinch of sea salt

SYRUP

200g sugar
240ml water
2 tablespoons honey
1 cinnamon stick

Preheat the oven to 180°C.

Grease 2 large baking sheets with vegetable oil.

In a mixing bowl, combine the filling ingredients and mix well, making sure the egg is fully incorporated.

Place the shredded filo dough in a large bowl. Drizzle the melted butter over the dough. Using your fingers, carefully loosen and separate the strands and turn to coat them evenly with melted butter.

Pick up a handful of dough with your fingertips and place it in the palm of your hand in a nest. Place about a tablespoon of filling into the middle of the dough in your palm. Fold the dough over the filling and roll until the remaining ends of dough are wrapped around. Place the rolled *kadaif* onto a prepared baking sheet and repeat with the remaining dough and filling.

Bake for 20 to 30 minutes until the *kadaif* rolls are golden brown. You may need to bake in batches if your oven can't fit both baking sheets at once.

Meanwhile, make the syrup: In a small saucepan, combine the syrup ingredients and bring to a boil over high heat. Reduce the heat to medium and simmer for 5 minutes, stirring once, until the sugar has dissolved. Remove from the heat and set aside to cool slightly.

Remove the *kadaif* from the oven and set aside to cool slightly. Drizzle a spoonful of warm syrup over each *kadaif* roll. Serve warm or at room temperature.

PITULITSI
FRITTERS

These fritters are traditionally made for Christmas Eve, New Year's Day or when visiting a newborn baby. They are a symbol of new beginning and new life. The dough itself is not very sweet, but a light dusting of powdered sugar adds just enough sweetness. They are best served fresh.

350ml warm water

7g fast action dried yeast

1 tablespoon plus ½ teaspoon sugar

500g plain flour

1 teaspoon sea salt

2 eggs, beaten

1 litre vegetable oil, for frying

Icing sugar, for dusting (optional)

Place the warm water in a small bowl and add the yeast and ½ teaspoon sugar. Cover the bowl with a plate and let stand until the yeast begins to foam, about 10 minutes.

Sift the flour into a large bowl and mix in 1 tablespoon sugar and the salt. Make a well in the centre of the flour and slowly pour in the yeast mixture and the eggs. Whisk the ingredients together to form a batter.

Cover the bowl with a large plate and set aside in a warm place to rise for 30 minutes. Remove the plate and punch down the dough. Cover and set aside for an additional 30 minutes. Remove and gently punch down the dough again.

In a large pot, heat the oil until it begins to shimmer and reaches a temperature of 180°C. Working in batches so as not to crowd the pot, carefully drop spoonfuls of batter into the hot oil. The dough will float and expand. Fry for 2 to 3 minutes on each side, until golden brown and cooked through. Using a slotted spoon, transfer the cooked fritters to a plate lined with paper towels to drain excess oil.

Let cool slightly before dusting with icing sugar. Serve immediately.

SUSAMLIJI
SESAME COOKIES

These are typically a celebration cookie and every Macedonian family I know makes them for special occasions. During the holidays, we always made platters of these cookies for our Macedonian neighbours and extended family.

5 eggs
120ml whole milk
120ml vegetable oil, plus extra
    for greasing
250g sugar
1 tablespoon baking powder
60ml freshly squeezed orange
    juice
700g plain flour, sifted, plus
    extra for dusting
40g sesame seeds

Using a stand mixer with the paddle attachment or hand mixer, mix together 4 of the eggs and the milk, oil, sugar, baking powder and orange juice. Slowly add the flour, mixing for a few minutes, until fully incorporated and a dough forms. Shape the dough into a ball and cover with cling film. Refrigerate for 20 minutes.

Preheat the oven to 180°C. Grease 2 large baking sheets with vegetable oil.

On a lightly floured work surface, portion out the dough into approximately 2-tablespoon-size pieces. Roll each piece of dough into a log about 1cm thick and about 10cm long. Fold each log in half and twist the ends together. Place the cookies onto the greased baking sheets, spacing them about 5cm apart.

In a small bowl, whisk the remaining egg to make an egg wash. Brush the cookies with the egg wash and sprinkle them generously with sesame seeds.

Bake the cookies for 15 to 20 minutes until golden brown. (You may need to do this in batches if your oven can't fit both baking sheets at once.)

SUTLIJACH
RICE PUDDING

This comforting dessert is almost effortless and full of flavour. Flavouring the milk with orange peel and cinnamon is the way my grandmother used to make it.

1 litre whole milk

200g short-grain rice

100g brown sugar

30g unsalted butter

¼ teaspoon sea salt

1 cinnamon stick

1 strip orange peel, peeled using a vegetable peeler

3 egg yolks

Ground cinnamon, for garnish

In a medium saucepan over high heat, stir together the milk, rice, sugar, butter, salt, cinnamon stick and orange peel. Bring to a boil and reduce the heat to medium. Simmer, covered, for 40 to 45 minutes, stirring often, until the rice is fully cooked. Discard the orange peel and cinnamon stick.

In a heat resistant bowl, whisk the egg yolks. Gradually ladle about 2 cups of the hot rice mixture into the egg yolks to temper the eggs.

Place the rice over low heat, and carefully pour the tempered eggs back into the pudding. Stir constantly for about 5 minutes.

Spoon the rice pudding into one large serving dish, or individual serving dishes or ramekins. Let it cool, then refrigerate until chilled. Garnish with a light dusting of cinnamon before serving.

BADEM KOLATSI
ALMOND COOKIES

There are many varieties of almond cookies made throughout the regions of Macedonia, but these are the style we made at home, particularly when we attended bridal and baby showers, where it is customary for guests to bring a dessert for the sweet table.

3 eggs
200g sugar
1 teaspoon vanilla extract
1 cup vegetable oil, plus extra for greasing
375g plain flour, sifted
2 teaspoons baking powder
¼ teaspoon bicarbonate of soda
½ teaspoon sea salt
140g flaked almonds, toasted

Preheat the oven to 180°C. Grease 2 large baking sheets with vegetable oil.

Using a stand mixer fitted with a paddle attachment or in a large bowl with a hand mixer, whisk the eggs. Pour in the sugar, vanilla and oil. Mix at medium speed for 2 minutes.

In a separate bowl, mix the flour, baking powder, bicarbonate of soda and salt. With the mixer running at medium speed, gradually mix the dry ingredients into the wet ingredients. Mix just until fully incorporated and a dough forms. Using a spatula, gently fold in 100g of the almonds.

Drop the dough onto the greased baking sheets in 2-tablespoon-size portions, spacing them about 5cm apart, since they will spread. Carefully sprinkle a few sliced almonds over each cookie and press them gently into the dough.

Bake for 20 to 22 minutes until the edges are golden brown. Bake in batches if your oven can't fit both baking sheets at once.

JOGURT TORTA

YOGURT CAKE

This light and delicate cake is only mildly sweet, with a bit of tang from the yogurt, giving it a sophisticated flavour despite its simplicity. I almost always have the ingredients on hand, so I make it often for my young children. For entertaining, I often serve it with a dollop of Slatko Od Chreshi (Cherry Preserves, page 262) and a glass of slivovitz, plum brandy. I recommend serving this cake warm.

113g unsalted butter at room temperature, plus extra for greasing
100g sugar
2 eggs
240ml plain full-fat Balkan yogurt (or any full-fat yogurt)
1 teaspoon lemon zest
1 teaspoon orange zest
250g plain flour
2 teaspoons baking powder
½ teaspoon bicarbonate of soda
½ teaspoon sea salt
Icing sugar, for dusting

Preheat the oven to 180°C. Grease a 23cm springform cake tin with butter.

Using a stand mixer fitted with the paddle attachment, or a large bowl and a hand mixer, cream the butter and sugar together until fluffy, about 4 minutes. Mix in the eggs, one at a time, until fully incorporated, about 1 minute. Fold in the yogurt and the lemon and orange zests. Set aside.

In a separate large bowl, sift together the flour, baking powder, bicarbonate of soda and salt. Carefully fold the dry ingredients into the wet ingredients just until a batter is formed. Be careful not to over-mix.

Pour the batter into the prepared cake tin, smoothing the top with a spatula. Bake for 30 minutes, or until the top is golden brown and a skewer inserted into the centre comes out clean.

Cool to room temperature. Remove the cake from the tin and dust with icing sugar before serving.

RAVANIJA
SYRUP CAKE

The use of semolina gives this cake an interesting texture and a mild flavour.
Pouring the syrup over the cake when it is hot out of the oven allows the sponge
to completely absorb the syrup, making this cake very moist and delicately sweet.

CAKE

6 room-temperature
    eggs, separated
50g sugar
180g semolina
¼ teaspoon sea salt
1 teaspoon vanilla extract
Butter, for greasing

SYRUP

700ml water
300g sugar
1 strip orange peel, peeled
    using a vegetable peeler
1 tablespoon orange juice
1 cinnamon stick

Preheat the oven to 180°C. Grease a 23 by 28cm cake tin with butter.

In a large bowl, whisk together the egg yolks and sugar until they become a creamy light yellow. Fold in the semolina, salt and vanilla extract.

In a stand mixer fitted with the whisk attachment, or in a large bowl using a hand mixer, whisk the egg whites until stiff peaks form.

Carefully fold about one-third of the egg whites into the yolk mixture. Pour the entire yolk mixture back into the bowl containing the egg whites and gently fold until just incorporated.

Pour the batter into the greased cake pan and carefully level using a spatula. Bake for 20 to 25 minutes, until a skewer inserted into the centre comes out clean.

Meanwhile, in a small saucepan, combine all of the syrup ingredients and bring to a boil over high heat. Reduce the heat to low and simmer for 10 to 15 minutes, or until the mixture has thickened and reduced by about half. Turn off the heat and discard the orange peel and cinnamon stick. Set aside to cool for 10 minutes.

Remove the cake from the oven and immediately slice diagonally to create diamond-shaped serving pieces. Pour the hot syrup all over the cake and allow it to cool completely before serving.

TULUMBI
SYRUP DOUGHNUTS

These were one of the first things I wanted to eat when we travelled to my parents' villages—my father is from Rula and my mother is from Bresnitza. These mini doughnuts are made with a choux pastry, or pâte à choux dough. They are found in nearly every bakery in Macedonia. A pastry bag with a star-shaped tip gives the Tulumbi their unmistakable shape. Freshly fried, they are soaked in a flavourful syrup and are best served right away.

SYRUP

240ml water
400g sugar
1 large orange peel
¼ teaspoon sea salt

DOUGHNUTS

240ml water
113g butter
1 tablespoon sugar
½ teaspoon sea salt
125g plain flour, sifted
3 eggs
1 litre vegetable oil, for deep-frying

In a small saucepan, combine all of the syrup ingredients and bring to a boil over high heat. Reduce the heat to medium and simmer for 5 minutes until the sugar and salt have dissolved completely. Remove the orange peel and set aside to cool.

In a medium saucepan, heat the vegetable oil over medium-high heat until it begins to shimmer, and reaches a temperature of 180°C.

In another medium saucepan placed over high heat, whisk together the water, butter, sugar and salt, and simmer, whisking constantly, until the sugar and salt are completely dissolved.

Reduce the heat to medium-low. Using a wooden spoon, stir the flour into the saucepan and continue to stir until the dough forms a ball, about 1 minute. Remove the pan from the heat and whisk in the eggs, one at a time.

Transfer the dough to a pastry bag fitted with a star tip. Squeeze out 5cm strips of dough into the hot oil, working in batches to avoid crowding the pan. Let them fry until golden brown, about 2 minutes on each side. Using a slotted spoon, remove the doughnuts from the oil and transfer to a plate lined with paper towels to drain excess oil.

Using a slotted spoon, dip the still-warm doughnuts into the syrup to fully coat them. Place on a serving dish and eat right away.

ZIMNICA

Preserves

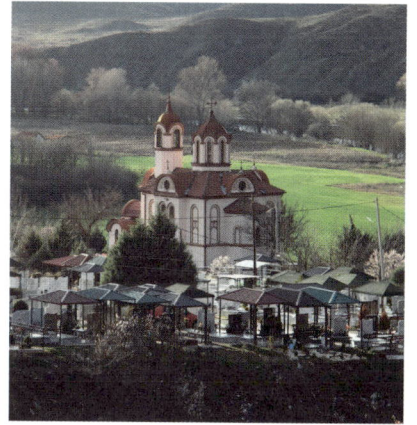

ZIMNICA
Preserves

Preserves are a very important element of the Macedonian table, and in Macedonia's past, a key part of survival. In the villages of Macedonia, storing food for the winter months was a communal family effort. Even during my childhood in Toronto, my family would get together every autumn and spend a weekend working to preserve the fruits and vegetables grown over the summer. We used preservation techniques that were passed down through generations, and took pride in not being wasteful.

Homemade jams, eaten with breads and tea, are a popular Macedonian breakfast. Pickled vegetables are typically enjoyed in the evenings, with a glass of rakija (fruit brandy). Dried fruits and vegetables are common snacks or incorporated into recipes. Homemade yogurt is a staple as well, and my parents would make it once a week.

TURSHIJA OD
PICKLED VEGETABLES
ZELENCHUK

In the autumn, my family spent weekends getting together to make preserves in preparation for the winter months. This medley of vegetables is great to have on hand, and we would quickly go through the jars. My Uncle Zivko was the best in the family at making Turshija. As a child, this was the only way my parents could get me to eat cauliflower.

½ head cauliflower, cut into 2.5–4cm florets

3 carrots, peeled, halved and cut into 5cm lengths

2 banana peppers (or use red peppers), sliced into 1cm thick rings

PICKLING BRINE

1½ teaspoons brown mustard seeds

480ml distilled white vinegar

6 garlic cloves, peeled

100g sugar

2 tablespoons salt

1 teaspoon black peppercorns

¼ teaspoon crushed chilli flakes

First make the pickling brine: In a stockpot over medium heat, toast the mustard seeds until fragrant, about 2 minutes. Pour in the vinegar and 350ml of water. Add the garlic, sugar, salt, peppercorns and chilli flakes. Increase the heat to high and bring to a boil.

If vegetables are to be consumed within 2 weeks, pack them in a clean jar or heatproof bowl and pour in the boiling brine to cover them fully. Set aside and cool, uncovered, until the brine reaches room temperature. Cover with a lid and refrigerate for at least 1 day before serving. Store in the refrigerator.

If preserving the pickles for longer-term storage, pack them into hot sterilised preserving jars. Pour in the hot brine leaving 1cm headspace at the top. Using a skewer or a chopstick, poke the vegetables down into the jars to remove any air bubbles. Place clean lids on top and screw on the tightening rings.

Half-fill a large pot with hot water and place the jars upright in the pot. Pour in enough hot water to submerge the jars fully and bring to a boil. Boil vigorously for 10 minutes. Carefully lift out the jars and let them cool completely.

Check to see that the lids have sunk down tightly. Refrigerate any jars that have not sealed and use within 2 weeks. Store the sealed jars in a cool dry place for at least 1 week before opening. After opening, store in the refrigerator and use within 2 weeks.

ZACHUVANI DOMATI

DRIED TOMATOES

Tomato plants seem to just explode with ripe tomatoes all at once. My family's garden is always so bountiful with tomatoes in the last few weeks of summer. This is a great way to utilise an abundant harvest. They are great to snack on, or you can serve them as a mezze or side dish, drizzled with a little olive oil.

1.8kg plum tomatoes, halved lengthwise

1 bulb garlic, skin on, cloves separated and halved

60ml extra-virgin olive oil

2 teaspoons sea salt

2 teaspoons freshly ground black pepper

Preheat the oven to 120°C.

Place all the ingredients in a large bowl and toss to coat.

Arrange the tomatoes on a large baking sheet in a single layer and roast for 2 hours. You may need to do this in batches.

Let cool and transfer to a jar or container. Store in the refrigerator and use within 1 week.

SLATKO OD
SMOKVI
FIG JAM

Fig jam is a common Macedonian breakfast or afternoon snack, served with tea and bread or sometimes cookies. It also makes an excellent addition to cheeseboards. Growing up in Canada, fresh figs were not readily available, so my family almost always bought fig jam imported from Macedonia. When I lived in Los Angeles, I was fortunate to have a beautiful mature fig tree in my backyard, and a fig tree was one of the first things I bought for our new home in Australia. Making this jam has become a yearly ritual I share with my daughter.

900g fresh figs, stems
  removed and quartered
220g brown sugar
240ml water
1 large lemon peel
1 large orange peel
2 cinnamon sticks
Juice of 1 lemon
1 teaspoon sea salt

In large stockpot over medium-high heat, stir together all of the ingredients, then lower the heat and simmer gently until the mixture has thickened and the figs break down, approximately 1½ hours. Remove the cinnamon stick and citrus peels, and allow the figs to cool for about 2 hours.

Using a food processor or immersion blender, purée the figs to your desired texture. Return to the pot and place over high heat until the jam begins to bubble. Transfer to sterilised mason jars, leaving 1cm headspace at the top.

Using a skewer or a chopstick, poke the fig jam down into the jars, removing any air bubbles. Place clean lids on top and screw on the tightening rings.

Half-fill a large pot with hot water and place the jars upright in the pot. Pour in enough hot water to submerge the jars fully and bring to a boil. Boil vigourously for 10 minutes. Carefully lift the jars out of the pot using tongs and let them cool completely.

Check to see that the lids have sunk down tightly. Refrigerate any jars that have not sealed and use within 2 weeks. Store sealed jars in a cool dry place. After opening, store in the refrigerator and use within 2 weeks.

SLATKO OD SLIVI
PLUM PRESERVES

These plum preserves are delicious as a sweet treat or as an accompaniment to cakes and breads. We often eat them straight from the jar or with a small drizzle of yogurt and chopped walnuts over the top. As kids, we also used to mix the syrup with sparkling water to make plum soda.

900g plums, pitted
   and quartered
200g sugar
60ml water
1 cinnamon stick
2 strips of orange peel
60ml brandy

In a medium stockpot, stir all the ingredients together over medium heat and bring to a boil. Reduce the heat and simmer for 25 minutes until the plums are tender. Some of the skin may loosen from the flesh.

Using a slotted spoon, transfer the plums to sterilised jars. Pour the hot cooking liquid over the plums in the jar, leaving 1cm headspace at the top. Using a skewer or a chopstick, poke the plums down into jars to remove any air bubbles. Place clean lids on top of the jars and screw on the tightening rings.

Half-fill a large pot with hot water and place the jars upright in the pot. Pour in enough hot water to submerge the jars fully and bring to a boil. Boil vigourously for 10 minutes. Carefully lift the jars out of the pot with tongs and let them cool completely.

Check to see that the lids have sunk down tightly. Refrigerate any jars that have not sealed and use within 2 weeks. Store sealed jars in a cool dry place. After opening, store in the refrigerator and use within 2 weeks.

SLATKO OD CHRESHI
CHERRY PRESERVES

Cherries are in season in the early summer in Macedonia and, like most fruits and vegetables, they grow in abundance. My parents have a thriving cherry tree in their backyard that my sister and I planted as children. These cherry preserves are sweet and tart with a bit of depth from the brandy. Spooned over yogurt, they make a great dessert or sweet breakfast.

1kg sweet dark cherries, pitted
70g brown sugar
100g sugar
Juice of 2 lemons
60ml brandy
½ teaspoon sea salt

In a medium saucepan, combine all of the ingredients and place over high heat. When the liquid starts to bubble, reduce the heat to medium and simmer for 1 hour, or until most of the liquid has evaporated and the mixture has begun to take on a thick consistency.

Transfer the cherries and their liquid to sterilised jars, leaving 1cm of headspace at the top. Using a skewer or a chopstick, poke the cherries down into the jars to remove any air bubbles. Place clean lids on top and screw on the tightening rings.

Half-fill a large pot with hot water and place the jars upright in the pot. Pour in enough hot water to submerge the jars fully and bring to a boil. Boil vigourously for 10 minutes. Carefully lift the jars out of the pot with tongs and let them cool completely.

Check to see that the lids have sunk down tightly. Refrigerate any jars that have not sealed and use within 2 weeks. Store sealed jars in a cool dry place. After opening, store in the refrigerator and use within 2 weeks.

JOGURT
YOGURT

Many Macedonians, my parents included, make homemade yogurt every few weeks. The flavour and texture of homemade yogurt is so beautiful, and it contains no preservatives. Making your own yogurt may sound intimidating, but it is really quite easy. My father taught me to test the temperature with a finger: "If you can hold your pinkie in the milk for 10 seconds before it gets too hot, that's how you know it's ready." An instant-read thermometer takes away the guesswork.

1.4 litres whole milk
6 tablespoons full-fat
  plain yogurt

Pour the milk into a large saucepan and place over medium-high heat. Bring the milk to a temperature of 82°C on an instant-read thermometer. The milk should be steaming, but barely bubbling. Be careful not to let it boil.

Carefully transfer the milk to a heatproof container and set aside to cool until the temperature reads 45°C.

Transfer 120ml of the heated milk into a small bowl and stir in the yogurt. Add the yogurt mixture back into the container with the milk and stir to incorporate.

Preheat the oven to 90°C and then turn it off.

Cover the heatproof container with a lid and wrap it in a towel to keep it warm. Place the wrapped container in the warm oven for 4 to 6 hours, without opening the oven door, until the yogurt has thickened.

Remove from the oven and refrigerate for a minimum of 2 hours before serving.

AUTHOR'S NOTE

If you think that you may have a food allergy or intolerance to any of the ingredients used in this book, it is a good idea to get specific dietary advice from your doctor or dietitian.

When preserving food for long-term storage, please consult the *USDA Complete Guide to Home Canning* for safe practices, and review the manufacturer's directions specific to your jars.

You can easily adjust the recipes to your personal taste. There are many variations to these recipes and different families and regions have their own adaptations.

All of the recipes in this book were created and tested using the following: sea salt, extra-virgin olive oil, unbleached plain flour, whole milk, large eggs and homemade meat and vegetable stocks (if you are using store-bought stocks, adjust the salt accordingly).

ACKNOWLEDGEMENTS

Oliver Fitzgerald To my love: This was fun! Thank you for your patience and support through this entire journey. The memories of us starting this book in our tiny rental with the world's smallest oven in Los Feliz are some of my favourites. It was a time of creativity and joy. We worked hard on this and I'm so proud we saw it through. You and I shared so much in the creation of this book and in our life together. Thank you for indulging me on my every whim regardless how "out there" it was. You are my biggest supporter and I wouldn't want to live my life without you.

Linda Nitsou To my mother, Linda: I truly couldn't have created this book without you. Thank you for all your endless hours helping me with testing recipes, chopping ingredients, editing my thoughts and consulting. It has been an incredible journey and you gave me the strength to see it through. I hope that I can be half of the mother to Kalina and Atteo as you have been to Christina and me.

George Nitsou To my father: Thank you for your devotion to us and ensuring we grew up to be educated women who had a strong understanding and connection to where we came from. Your never-ending thirst for knowledge is an inspiration to us and your guidance in the culture and historical background of Macedonia helped me immensely in writing this book.

Christina McIsaac Thank you for all your love and support. You are the strongest and hardest working woman I know. I would be lost without you and am so grateful that you are my sister.

Sophie Litsas Teta Sofa, your knowledge is like a portal from the old country to the new. You have guided me so much through the trials of this book. You helped me paint a picture of our heritage.

Hristina To my darling friend: you are a ray of sunshine in my life and I thank you for always cheering me on. You understand my determination and have never told me to slow down, but rather pushed me to be greater, which is always what I need to hear in times of doubt. Our friendship blossomed into family and I adore you.

Suzanna Bojadjieva Thank you for helping me connect to the stories and traditions of Macedonia. Thank you for broadening my knowledge; it has been a wonderful gift.

Dr. Christina Kramer, Professor of Slavic and Balkan Languages at the University of Toronto
Thank you for your work in helping me to ensure the translations in the book are accurate. You are beloved by the Macedonian community.

Meto Koloski, President of the United Macedonia Diaspora in the US Thank you, Meto, for your endless support and encouragement on the creation of this book. Your constant devotion to the culture and prosperity of Macedonians everywhere is truly an inspiration. I'm so proud of our friendship and proud of you, because your job at UMD is not easy, and you never waver in your determination.

Jake Rivera Thank you for your work on and support for this book. From our first meeting in Silver Lake you supported this project and were unceasingly patient with my many additions until we got it just right.

INDEX

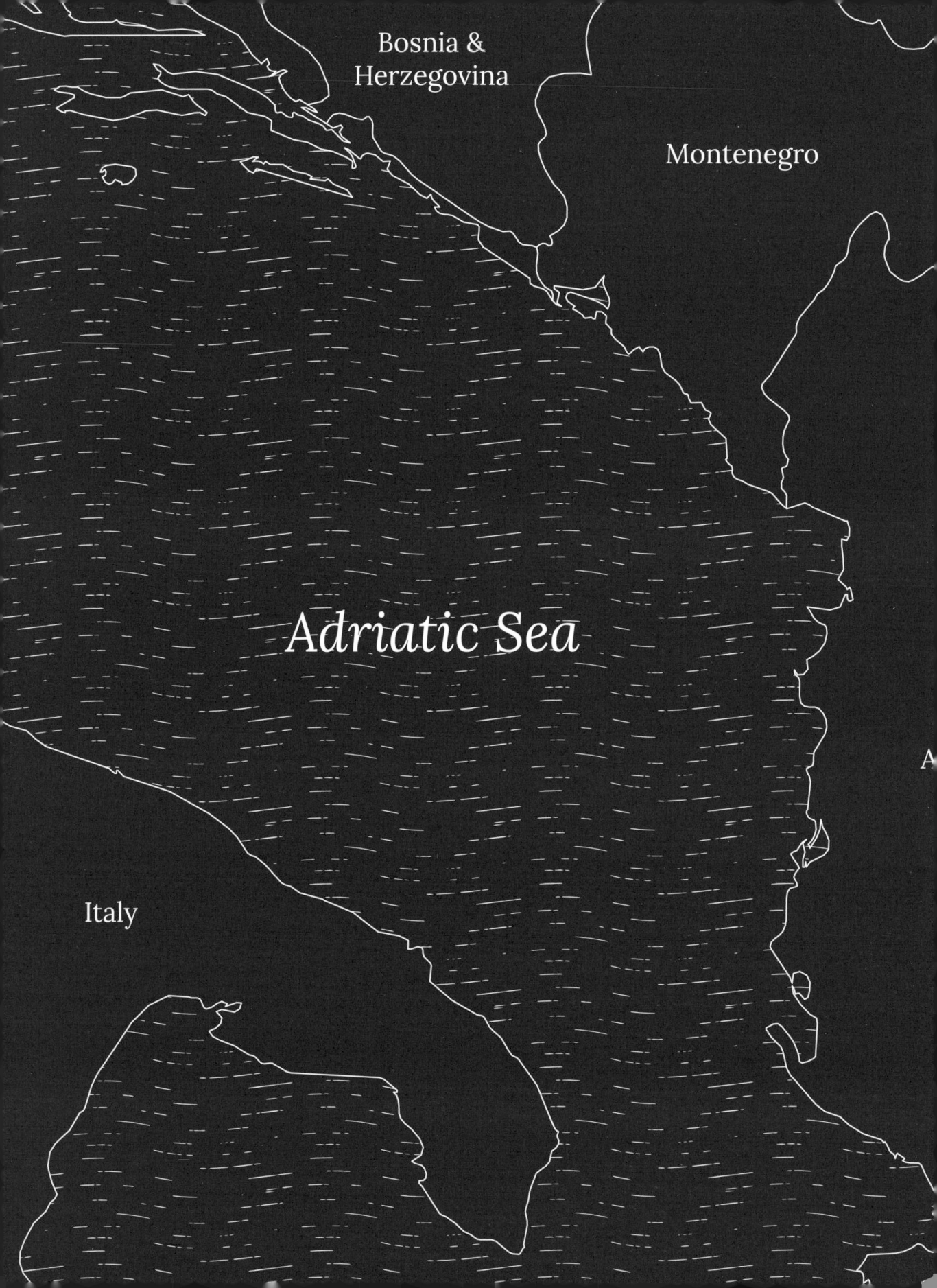

Bosnia &
Herzegovina

Montenegro

Adriatic Sea

A

Italy